Handbook on How to Build Superintendent-Board Relationships

Handbook on How to Build Superintendent-Board Relationships

John Maloy

ROWMAN & LITTLEFIELD
Lanham • Boulder • New York • London

Published by Rowman & Littlefield
An imprint of The Rowman & Littlefield Publishing Group, Inc.
4501 Forbes Boulevard, Suite 200, Lanham, Maryland 20706
www.rowman.com

86-90 Paul Street, London EC2A 4NE, United Kingdom

Copyright © 2025 by John Maloy

All rights reserved. No part of this book may be reproduced in any form or by any electronic or mechanical means, including information storage and retrieval systems, without written permission from the publisher, except by a reviewer who may quote passages in a review.

British Library Cataloguing in Publication Information Available

Library of Congress Cataloging-in-Publication Data

Names: Maloy, John, 1958– author.
Title: Handbook on how to build superintendent-board relationships / John Maloy.
Description: Lanham, Maryland : Rowman & Littlefield, [2025] | Includes bibliographical references. | Summary: "How to Build Superintendent-Board Relationships provides valuable strategies on how to navigate the dynamics of superintendent-board working relationships; highlights successful practices for addressing conflict and dysfunction; and serves as a template for successful superintendent-board governance and operations"—Provided by publisher.
Identifiers: LCCN 2024042438 (print) | LCCN 2024042439 (ebook) | ISBN 9781475874921 (cloth) | ISBN 9781475874938 (paperback) | ISBN 9781475874945 (epub)
Subjects: LCSH: School superintendents—Professional relationships. | School board members—Professional relationships. | Conflict management. | Communication in education.
Classification: LCC LB2831.72 .M35 2025 (print) | LCC LB2831.72 (ebook) | DDC 371.2/011—dc23/eng/20241017
LC record available at https://lccn.loc.gov/2024042438
LC ebook record available at https://lccn.loc.gov/2024042439

∞™ The paper used in this publication meets the minimum requirements of American National Standard for Information Sciences—Permanence of Paper for Printed Library Materials, ANSI/NISO Z39.48-1992.

To my precious grandchildren, Banks and Collins, who I hope through love and inspiration will always chase their dreams.

Acknowledgments

The world is a better place thanks to people who want to develop and lead others. What makes it even better are people who share the gift of their time to mentor. Dr. Leonard Burrello and Dr. Ron Barnes have been mentors in my life and have influenced and inspired me along my career path. Without their support, encouragement, and critical review of the manuscript, this book would not have been possible.

I need to thank my daughter, Dr. Megan Maloy Shepley, who graciously assisted with all things—Google forms, documents, collaboration, and spreadsheets. Megan's participation proved very beneficial and timely.

Also, I wish to thank my parents, John and Gail Maloy, for instilling in me the love of learning and for modeling that hard work is the key to success. Their support allowed me to be the first member of the Maloy extended family to complete college and earn a degree.

Finally, I would like to thank my best friend and love of my life, my wife, Lori. She has always been my beacon of light in the darkness and has shown me and others what it means to be kind and compassionate while serving others in need. She read drafts of my work and provided her keen eye for details and revisions.

Contents

Acknowledgments — vii
Foreword — xi
Preface — xiii

1. Historical Perspective — 1
2. Interviewing, Hiring, and Succeeding — 5
3. Negotiating the Superintendent's Contract — 13
4. Working to Develop Trust and Mutual Respect — 21
5. Establishing Clear Roles — 31
6. Building Communication Pathways — 35
7. Realizing Ideologically Driven Politics — 39
8. Creating Strong Community Relations — 43
9. Addressing Dysfunctional Leadership — 47
10. Partnering during Teacher Contract Negotiations — 51
11. Addressing Conflict/Power Struggles — 57
12. Dealing with the Media — 61
13. Working with Standing Committees — 65
14. Balancing Work and Home Life — 69
15. Creating a Framework for Good Governance — 73

16	Utilizing Data-Driven Decision-Making	81
17	Engaging Administrative Team/Cabinet Members	85
18	Managing Crises	89
19	Keeping Your Bags Packed	95
20	Thinking about Your Legacy	101
21	Analyzing Superintendent Survey Data	103

Appendix A: Thought-Provoking Scenarios	107
Appendix B: Author's Thoughts on the Scenarios	113
Appendix C: Questions for Practicing Superintendents and Data Summary Table	123
Bibliography	129
Index	135
About the Author	143

Foreword

Since their inception, public schools have been the site of a struggle. It should be no surprise, then, that once the enterprise of schooling became big and complex enough that it needed someone to oversee it, that job, the superintendency, has been the site of struggle, not between public schools and the public they serve but between the superintendent and almost everyone: the boards of education who ultimately oversee the schools and the superintendent, the community the schools serve, and the schools and everyone in them.

The superintendency is also one of the most fulfilling jobs in education, which is a claim I make from experience. It is fulfilling because of the impact it can have on students as there is always *more* to do and *more* to learn. No one outgrows the superintendency.

Taken together, a job that is historically challenging and becoming more challenging all the time and at the same time one of the most fulfilling jobs an educator can have, what's needed is a handbook that parses out the details of the job and offers strategies for surviving and even flourishing in the role. Those two accomplishments, surviving and flourishing, must happen first in the superintendent's relationship with the board of education. Dr. John Maloy's *Handbook on How to Build Superintendent-Board Relationships* addresses a significant gap in the literature that superintendent candidates are exposed to in their preparation programs. On the one hand, we read that every variable in the relationship between the board and superintendent is statistically significant, but on the other hand, Dr. Maloy's research indicates that 97.5 percent of superintendents say that their relationship with their board of education is important while only one-third of them reported that they felt prepared. The superintendency cannot be a "learn-on-the-job" job.

This book is not just for superintendents. Dr. Maloy rightly situates his book in the relationship between superintendents and their boards, and board members should read it to better understand the role of the superintendent and the unique challenges of that position, and more importantly, to understand their role in making that relationship successful and in so doing make the schools they were elected to serve more successful.

Of course, no one book can fill that gap. For the sake of everyone who cares about public education, and that should be all of us, and for the sake of everyone who aspires to serve as superintendent—and we need more of those people and from every background—and for those future superintendents who aspire to serve longer than the current average of four years, this book is hopefully one that starts a movement among scholars and practitioners to flatten the learning curve of the superintendency. Until then, read and study Dr. Maloy's book.

Dr. Bruce Law
Superintendent, Highland Park Township,
High School District, 113
Highland Park, IL

Preface

"Success is not something to wait for, it is something to work for."

Henry Wadsworth Longfellow

Longfellow was an American poet and educator. He wrote many lyric poems known for musicality and often presenting stories of mythology and legend. He became the most popular American poet of his day.

A significant portion of a school district's success depends on the performance of its superintendent and board. Several studies have examined the dynamics between superintendents and school boards, and most conclude that a positive relationship between these two parties ultimately drives the successful governance of a district.[1] The superintendent and school board relationship was emphasized as vital by Marshall and Ulrich.[2] According to their study, every single variable they analyzed that was related to a superintendent's relationship with the school board was statistically significant, even when including other variables such as a superintendent's gender or size of a district. To illustrate the importance of a collaborative superintendent-board relationship, Carter and Cunningham[3] found that the primary reason for superintendents leaving their districts was due to the lack of support from and conflicting relationships with school board members. Further, Ray[4] stated, "A superintendent can possess all the necessary competencies to be an effective leader, but it is the school board's perception of success that really matters."

With four decades of experience in public education, including fourteen years serving as a superintendent, the author's rationale for this book grew from observing, living, and working through the complexities of the superintendent's role and the challenges of developing and maintaining a positive working relationship with elected board members; the results of a superintendent survey addressing superintendent-school board relationships; concern for the tenure of superintendents and why they leave their roles; and the impending future superintendent shortage. In addition, my experience and the survey found that superintendent preparation programs were often geared toward academics but lacked practical application with regard to superintendent-school board relations.

The superintendency has evolved over time. The role of school superintendents is broad. It can be rewarding, but the decisions they make can also be especially difficult and taxing. It takes an exceptional person with a unique skill set to be an effective school superintendent. While in the past, a superintendent could be called a successful superintendent by managing items such as books, bonds, buildings, and budgets, in the twenty-first century, a superintendent must be an expert in things such as collaboration, community building, communication, and curricular choices. As the role and expectations of the superintendency change, the pressures also tend to change and become more complex, thus the need for a collaborative relationship between the superintendent and the school board intensifies.

To verify the value of importance practicing superintendents placed on the superintendent-school board relationship, a survey was developed to obtain superintendents' feedback. The survey was randomly distributed to 858 superintendents with 118 superintendents returning the survey. The overall response rate was 13.8 percent. When superintendents were asked how many hours in their course of study were designated toward explaining or preparing them for the importance of superintendents-school board relationships, 56.8 percent of the superintendents stated that 4 hours or less were designated toward explaining or preparing them for the importance of superintendents-school board relationships; however, 97.5 percent of the superintendents rated the superintendent-school board relationships as being most important or very important in attaining the school district's vision and mission. Consequently, 78.8 percent of superintendents responded that since becoming a superintendent they spend a minimum of 2 hours per month (minimum of 24 hours per year) engaged in activities to assist in improving the superintendent-school board relationships.

While the superintendent may not be visible in his/her day-to-day roles, the superintendent's leadership can significantly influence the culture and success of a school district. Changes in leadership can create uncertainty and affect school climate, which in turn impact everyone involved in the educational process. Therefore, maintaining a consistent course of action is a prerequisite for success in schools. Frequent turnover in district leadership disrupts learning and evaluation for students and staff. The longer the superintendent stays in his/her role, while maintaining teacher stability, the more consistent the learning and evaluation become. With the average tenure of a superintendent lasting less than four years, each change in leadership creates a replacement or redirection of core practices and reforms disrupting the stability of leadership for staff, students, and the entire school community.[5] It is no wonder that teachers resist change that comes from a revolving door of central office leadership.

When the superintendent-school board relationship is strained, the superintendent turnover is increased. The concern for superintendent turnover is validated by several studies that reveal the tenure of superintendents is between 2.5 and 6.5 years.[6,7,8] As with any organization, a high turnover rate at the leadership level results in a lack of continuity of policy implementation and enforcement and contributes to a general atmosphere of chaos and lack of direction. Furthermore, several studies and superintendent surveys found superintendents leave a district due to a poor relationship with the school board. A conflicted and mistrusting relationship between the superintendent and school board is one pressure that can result in a high superintendent turnover rate.

A survey conducted by the education company EAB[9] on the number of superintendents contemplating leaving their position found that 46 percent of superintendents are considering or planning to leave their role in the next two to three years and that more than a third of experienced superintendents, those with six or more years of tenure, are planning on retiring within that time frame. It also found that eight in ten superintendents say that navigating politically divisive conversations is the most challenging part of their job today, which contributes to the superintendents' desire to leave their role. Today's educational landscape is marked by complex issues related to challenging state and national standards in the context of a continuing economic recovery and increasing demands for accountability while a variety of educational options are growing in competition with local school districts with access to public dollars. With public schools feeling state and national pressure to improve, exceptional leadership has never been more important. Public education is facing a shrinking pool of talented candidates for the superintendency and there is a groundswell of superintendents expressing their sense of isolation, concern, and even discontent with their profession. Consequently, if and when superintendents make the decision to leave, school districts will struggle to find candidates with the necessary talent and passion. In these situations, superintendents who choose to stay will be constantly overwhelmed with requirements to do more or inexperienced candidates will be pressed into roles without the preparation and support needed to lead their school districts through ongoing challenges.

According to an article published in the *American Educational Research Journal*[10] in 2012, the story of school superintendent turnover is a well-known one:

> Energetic new leader assumes position with plans for revitalization, only to clash with a dysfunctional school board or impatient community and move-on to greener pastures before the plan can be fully carried out, leaving the district once again searching for the next great leader bearing the necessary comprehensive reform plan.

The loss of continuity can certainly lead to low morale among staff members, cause others in the district to become anxious, negatively impact the implementation of programs, and bring a quick halt to innovative projects. Also, districts with frequent superintendent turnover can have trouble attracting and retaining a qualified superintendent. Finding candidates willing to commit long term is difficult if one of the factors contributing to the high turnover rate is a tumultuous superintendent-board relationship.

Despite many years of experience spent as classroom teachers, principals, and central office administrators, few superintendents claim that they were well-prepared to be a school district superintendent when they accepted their first contract. Likewise, the survey revealed that when superintendents were asked on a scale from 1 to 5, with 1 being not prepared and 5 being very well prepared, how well prepared they were for their first superintendent position, 67 percent of superintendents responded that they were not prepared, slightly prepared, or somewhat prepared. Most of them stated that from day one on the job, they continued to learn something new about their role each and every day. Although aspiring and current superintendents typically learn many strategies and leadership skills through these opportunities, rarely do they learn how to work with school boards. In general, many superintendents find they do not know how to prioritize their work and ensure that board members become an important part of their work. Effective superintendent-board relationships are critical to student achievement and district progress, yet the tenure of superintendents continues to be relatively short, especially in large and urban school districts.[11]

Superintendent-school board relationships are more important than ever as their leadership teams grapple with the demands placed on their districts from state legislatures and federal government initiatives and their own communities' aspirations. The board does not work in a vacuum. It is the interaction or relationship between the superintendent and board that ultimately sets the stage for success or tension in the district. When the partnership of the superintendent and board works successfully, both parties understand state and federal mandates as well as a multitude of issues including curriculum, instruction, staffing, budgeting, operations, and, most importantly, student achievement. Both entities understand the community in which they live and work, and they understand the ways that public education reflects the values of today while preparing students for the world of tomorrow.

Therefore, the purpose of writing this book is to help superintendents develop effective strategies in working with school board members which will create successful school district governance teams. Also, first-time superintendents and veterans moving on to another school district will find lessons to guide them throughout the day-to-day operations and help them avoid many opportunities for adversity. School board members will find the book helpful in opening their eyes to the importance of their interaction and relationship with the superintendent as they set the stage for district progress and success. Additionally, the book will contribute to debunking superintendent-board relations and will serve all readers as a practical handbook and guide to successful leadership and governance. Finally, after reflecting on my forty-year career in education and educational leadership, I am hopeful that sharing experiences and offering some insights will assist both the designated leader and board members in guiding and counseling those considering a track in educational leadership and those already serving in this role.

The book provides an opportunity for superintendents and school board members to reflect, review, discuss, and implement appropriate role and responsibilities for the purpose of developing a successful and effective superintendent-school board relationship which will only enhance both entities' ability to attain the district's goals, values, and mission.

NOTES

1. Alsbury, Thomas (2008). Hitting a moving target: How politics determines the changing roles of superintendents and school boards. In *Handbook of education politics, and policy*. 2nd Edition. New York, NY: Routledge, pp. 37–61.

2. Marshall, Joanne M. and Ulrich, Jesse D. (2022). *How to keep your superintendent: Board factors related to superintendent turnover*. National School Boards Association. http://works.bepress.com/joanne_marshall/44/

3. Carter, Gene R. and Cunningham, William G. (1997). *The American school superintendent: Leading in an age of pressure*. San Francisco, CA: Jossey-Bass.

4. Ray, H. A. (2003). *ISLLC administrator competencies: A comparison of perceptions among superintendents, school board presidents, and principals* (Doctoral dissertation). Dissertation Abstracts International.

5. Hanover Research (2020). *Effective superintendent & school board collaboration*. Washington, DC: Hanover Research, District Administration Practices.

6. Glass, Thomas E. (1992). *The study of the American school superintendency*. Arlington, VA: American Association of School Administrators.

7. Kowalski, Theodore J., McCord, Robert S., Petersen, George J., Young, I. Phillip, and Ellerson, Noelle M. (2011). *The American school superintendent: 2010 decennial study.* Lanham, MD: Rowman & Littlefield.

8. Metzger, Christa (1997). Involuntary turnover of superintendents. *Thrust for Educational Leadership*, 26(4), pp. 20–22.

9. EAB Education Consulting (2022). *Voice of the superintendent survey.* Washington, DC: EAB Education Consulting.

10. Grissolm, Jason A. and Andersen, Stephanie (2012). Why *superintendents turn over. American Educational Research Journal*, 49(6), pp. 1146–1180. https://doi.org/10.3102/0002831212462622.

11. Endie, D. C. (2019). *Building a high-impact board-superintendent partnership: 11 critical questions you need to answer.* Lanham, MD: Rowan and Littlefield Publishers.

Chapter 1

Historical Perspective

"Those who don't know history are destined to repeat it."

Edmund Burke

Burke was an Irish political leader and philosopher widely regarded as the philosophical founder of conservatism.

School boards have been responsible for governing schools since the seventeenth century in U.S. history. Boston created the first comprehensive system of public schools in America during the colonial period. The governing body at the time was a school committee of twelve elected members. There was one member for each ward of the city. Eventually, nearly every city and state adopted the Boston pattern of governance with the committee actually administering the schools.[1]

During the 1800s school systems became larger and the task of governing the schools became more time-consuming thus requiring greater skills. Because of this, school boards began to hire technical experts in the field of education called superintendents to administer the schools.[2] By 1890, almost every major American city school board employed a superintendent.

Early superintendents functioned differently from the way most function today. Usually, the board continued to maintain the power in the relationship and the superintendent was an aide to the board. The relationship between the superintendent and board evolved with superintendents assuming more power and responsibility as time passed.

As superintendents assumed more power, conflict between superintendents and boards became more common, and by 1872, conflict over how much authority the board and the superintendent should maintain became more divisive and intense. Superintendents wanted more prestige and the power to decide appointments of personnel and the details of expenditures within a budget established by the board. Superintendents wanted to be appointed for longer terms and to be viewed as the chief executives of the school district with veto power over the board. In addition, a study by the Department of Superintendents of the National Education Association criticized boards for their lack of competence in educational matters.

The differences that arose during the latter part of the 1800s continue today and are the basis for the tension which is part of the superintendent-school board relationships. Hanover Research[3] found in its study that 20 percent of superintendents believe that boards are a major obstacle in carrying out their jobs in a professional manner and 70 percent of superintendents believe that boards should act solely on the superintendent's recommendations in hiring personnel while only 20 percent of board members agree. Further evidence of the tension between superintendents and boards is reported by McGonagill.[4] He found that superintendents and boards compete for control of policymaking and implementation which undermines the ability of both the superintendent and board to formulate initiatives and to put them into action. Finally, Merz[5] summarized the tension, conflict, and the relationship between the superintendent and school board this way:

> *School boards are lay groups that exercise policy-making power over an institution the working of which has at least, a quasi-technological base. But then, everybody has been to school and knows how things should be done. Superintendents are hired for their expertise as educators and managers. They are assumed to really know how things should be done. However, leaders or not, they are employees and in a very real way their welfare depends on keeping the board happy or minimally unhappy. The bind then goes something like this. We have an expert, by definition, who cannot exercise his or her expertise on matters of real substance without getting the support and confirming decisions of a number of non-experts (the school board) who are influenced by a host of other non-experts (the community). The latter group, for many intents and purposes, are the same kind of people who are on the board and, therefore, also know how things should be done. Further, this global situation is a stable one since in many systems there is frequent turnover in board membership, presenting the superintendent with the likelihood of having to deal with a new group of non-experts every other year or so and sometimes more often.*

NOTES

1. Cistone, Peter J. (ed.) (1975). *Understanding school boards: Problems and prospects*. Lexington, MA: D.C. Heath & Company, Lexington Books, p. 304.

2. Ziegler, L. Harmon, Jennings, M. Kent, and Peak, G. Wayne (1974). *Governing American schools: Political interactions in local school districts*. North Scituate, MA: Duxbury Press, p. 269.

3. Hanover Research (2014). *Effective board and superintendent collaboration*. Washington, DC: Hanover Research, District Administration Practices.

4. McGonagill, Grady (1987). Board/staff partnership: The key to effectiveness of state and local boards. *Phi Delta Kappan International,* 69(1), September, pp. 65–68.

5. Merz, Carol S. (1986). Conflict and *frustration* for *school board members. Urban Education,* 20, pp. 397–418.

Chapter 2

Interviewing, Hiring, and Succeeding

"Believe you can and you're halfway there."

Theodore Roosevelt

Roosevelt was an American politician, statesman, conservationist, naturalist, and writer who served as the twenty-sixth president of the United States from 1901 to 1909. Historians and political scientists rank him as one of the greatest presidents in American history.

According to the National School Boards Association,[1] arguably, the most important responsibility of a board of education is the hiring of a superintendent. Typically, board members are expected to make this important decision without having had experience as a superintendent or even a clear understanding of the day-to-day requirements of the job. Thus, frequently the situation is a group of underprepared volunteers making the most important decision they can make for their school community.

The process of hiring a superintendent is normally an attempt to determine a "fit." First, board members attempt to estimate the level of job fit. In other words, the board attempts to evaluate whether an applicant possesses the qualifications for the job that corresponds to the job requirements. Second, the board attempts to determine the level of person-organization fit. Does the applicant have the personality, values, and interests that correspond to the district's organizational values and culture?

The primary means used to make these determinations of "fit" are interviews. The interview process can result in a wide range of outcomes. In other words, a poorly designed and conducted interview will provide very little insight into the applicant's potential to perform in the organization. On the other hand, even though the best selection methods will sometimes lead to bad hiring decisions, more valid methods will dramatically increase the proportion of good hiring decisions.

Once an initial interview pool is selected, the board should schedule and conduct screening interviews. The screening interview should be a shortened version of a second, more comprehensive interview. The purpose of the screening interview is to validly and fairly narrow the larger pool so that an in-depth interview will occur with only the most promising candidates.

Of course, the types of questions asked matter. The questions used must accurately capture the job requirements of the superintendent. To achieve this goal, the questions should be based on the Professional Standards for School Leaders.[2]

Decades of employment-interview research have highlighted the value of structured interviews. Better hiring decisions are made if the questions are prepared in advance, all interviewees are asked the same questions in the same order, and anchored rating scales are used to score and compare applicant's responses. This type of systematic, standardized approach reduces the risk of biases, errors, and personal preferences.

The comprehensive interview contains both more and different questions designed to assess an applicant's ability to handle the major job performance categories.[3] The process for completing the comprehensive interview is largely the same as the process that was used to complete the screening interview. One difference is that a comprehensive interview could contain the option of requiring the candidate to complete a performance task. The board should decide in advance if they are going to require completion of one of these tasks. If the decision is made to require the completion of a performance task, it must be the same task for all candidates.

Using a process like the one articulated will greatly increase the chances that the school board will select the most appropriate candidate, but there is not just one way to search for a superintendent. The major choices are whether to hire from within the district or to recruit from outside the district. It is possible that in the district's succession plan, an experienced associate superintendent is a natural fit, who already has established relationships, knows about the challenges and successes in the district, and is ready to assume the superintendent's role.

Other searches may be more involved and expensive as school boards regularly contract with a professional search firm to lead the superintendent search. Most school board members do not have the skills and background required to hire a superintendent or negotiate a multiyear contract. Consequently, school boards usually send out an official Request for Proposal (RFP) and then select from the search firms who respond. The RFP outlines the search firm's scope of work, which includes the school board's requirements as well as other activities which include to

1. Design a leadership profile.
2. Create advertisements for the open position.
3. Generate a position description with desired qualifications.
4. Solicit applications nationally.
5. Assist with logistics of finalists interviews.
6. Develop a community engagement process.
7. Ensure a satisfactory conclusion to the searches.

The proposals submitted highlight the search firm's expertise and past placements and describe how it intends to meet the district's needs. A fee for services is included as well. Most school boards interview the preferred firms in public at a school board meeting and vote to hire and approve the search firm's contract in an open session.

After the search firm has surveyed and interviewed key stakeholders, it writes a description of the district's needs and strengths in order to advertise the open position. The search firm then prescreens applicants for those that best match the district's needs and assembles a portfolio of candidates to present to the school board. The board, in a series of properly noticed closed-session meetings, screens resumes and related materials and selects four to six candidates to attend a first round of interviews. Based on the district's needs, the search firm assists the school board in composing questions for the interview process.

The challenge for the board of education is finding a balance between maintaining all candidates' confidentiality and appeasing the community and media who have a desire to know everything about the process and candidates. It can be a slippery slope as candidates may not be ready to signal to a current employer that they are ready to explore another opportunity, while the board may want to be transparent with the community and receive affirmation of its decisions and processes as they move through the timeline.

Also, serious thought should be given to student participation. Without a doubt, students should be involved in this important hiring decision and invited to be participants in the interview process where it is appropriate. Interviews usually occur in closed sessions and are confidential. Consequently, the students who are selected to participate must demonstrate mature behavior and be willing and able to maintain confidentiality.

Recker[4] points out that in some cases, reaching a consensus on a superintendent hire can be difficult as board members go through a process of elimination and compromise. Sometimes a simple majority is the best a school board can do. However, it is essential to give the new superintendent the benefit of unanimous support. The superintendent and school board act as a governance team, and the strength of the superintendent-board relationship is important to the outcomes of the governance team. Research shows that with very few exceptions, the longer a superintendent stays in the district, the better students perform.

Just as school boards must prepare and plan for the interview process, it is crucial that candidates prepare for the interview to ensure that they are able to exhibit their skills and experience effectively. To help candidates prepare for an interview, Krosel et al.[5] offer some suggestions:

1. Research the school thoroughly. This will help the candidate understand the district's mission, values, and goals. The process will assist the candidate in identifying the district's strengths and weaknesses, which can help tailor responses during the interview.
2. Review the job description carefully. This will help the candidate understand the responsibilities and requirements of the position and prepare the candidate for questions related to his/her experience and qualifications.
3. Review common interview questions for superintendents and prepare responses.
4. Practice responses to common interview questions with a friend. This will help the candidate feel more confident and comfortable during the interview.
5. Dress professionally for the interview. This will help the candidate make a good first impression and show that the candidate takes the interview seriously.
6. Bring copies of your resume, cover letter, and other related documents. This will help the candidate provide additional information if needed.
7. Prepare a list of questions to ask the interviewers. This will show the candidate is interested in the position and has done the research.

When the candidate prepares for the interview, he/she realizes several benefits. The candidate improves his/her comfort level heading into an interview and by knowing many of the questions they might ask and understanding how to answer them, the candidate relieves stress and increases confidence.

Without question, the face-to-face interview is a crucial step in the hiring process for new superintendents. A strong resume and good references can make an interview more likely, but even the strongest resumes and recommendations rarely can overcome a weak, mistake-prone interview. The following are a few of the most common interview missteps a superintendent candidate should avoid:

1. Talking too much. It can be tempting for a candidate to tell all that he/she knows about the topic of the question. However, while the answer continues to unfold, board members are thinking about how much time

they have allotted for the interview and the number of questions yet to come. As a result, the candidate should focus on the essential aspects of his/her answer, including an example or two, but the candidate should limit his/her response to about two minutes. The candidate can also help the situation by asking before the interview starts how much time has been allotted. This information will help you to gauge the length of the candidate's responses in light of the time available.
2. Failing to become familiar with the district. When a candidate fails to become informed of current local initiatives or circumstances, it sends a message of disregard and inattentiveness to the position.
3. Focusing on what you would do rather than what you have done. Responses and examples focused on proposed future actions risk sounding less about experience and more like speculation. A response about real experiences usually carries more weight than future-focused hypotheses about how you would handle a situation.
4. Neglecting to make eye contact. The candidate does not want to lose communication contact with the interviewers; therefore, a good strategy is to maintain eye contact with the interviewers until the question is completely answered.
5. Failing to fully listen to questions. The interview environment can be filled with pressure making it more challenging to listen effectively. However, failing to hear and respond appropriately to interview questions makes it difficult to have a successful interview. If the candidate is struggling, consider jotting reminder notes, ask for clarification of the question, or ask to have the question repeated.
6. Allowing nervous habits to appear. Clicking a pen, playing with your hair, or other behaviors that signal nervousness can be distracting to the point where they overshadow what the candidate can bring to the position.
7. Criticizing current or previous employers and colleagues. Many boards conclude that if a candidate is willing to criticize past employers, a board member may be next. Further, board members are likely to suspect that the situation may have more than one side and that the candidate's responsibility is not being acknowledged. The old adage, "If you cannot say something nice, say nothing." is good advice for interviews.

If the candidate commits one or two of these interviewing mistakes, the candidate should not be too concerned as most of the mistakes are not fatal by themselves. However, avoid allowing them to pile up. Too many mistakes in the same interview can be difficult to overcome regardless of the skill set and experience the candidate possesses.

Beginning a new superintendency is a challenge and an opportunity. There is usually a very short honeymoon period for a new superintendent. The board wants to be proven correct that it made a good hire. Also, the superintendent wants to validate the board's confidence in his/her ability to build upon the district's work and make improvements where necessary. Relationship building during the first few months is paramount to the superintendent's success. The first few months of being a new superintendent are busy ones as he/she needs to listen, learn, and communicate. The new superintendent should talk to as many stakeholders as possible as he/she will learn by listening and the people with whom he/she interacts will feel valued. As with any leadership role, high-performing superintendents must strike a balance between not acting too quickly while demonstrating quick, visible, and measurable actions.

Many new superintendents also arrive with a set of preconceptions and biases—beliefs that they can turn things around, get things moving, or save the district from some dramatic and negative fate that would materialize had they not accepted the position as superintendent. This kind of belief makes them appear arrogant, and it's that arrogance that can contribute to new superintendents making classic mistakes. For those newly hired superintendents and others who want to avoid some of these classic mistakes, Kerrin and Cushing[6] (2001) offer some strategies:

1. Always be from where you are. The superintendent's words and actions should honor the work, thinking, and plans of your new colleagues. Talking about "how it was done in the school district from where he/she came" from is a non-starter. These kinds of statements and attitudes dishonor the work that's gone on before the new superintendent arrived.
2. Seek multiple perspectives and practice active listening. Before offering advice, recommendations, or guidance, the superintendent should collect data from enough sources with a variety of perspectives to develop a thorough understanding of the issues. Before suggesting action, the superintendent should seek out both confirming and disconfirming evidence for his/her conclusions. Also, try to understand the consequences of any change might have for the organization, both in the present and future.
3. Practice possibility thinking. Try to avoid win-lose actions and language. Find a way to be more inclusive and to do the seemingly impossible.
4. Adopt a value-added perspective. When the superintendent shares his/her ideas, vision, or action plans, he/she should be certain to note how each builds on the work that's happened before. Remember, recognizing someone else's contribution will doubly repay the superintendent.

5. Remember timing is everything. Although the new superintendent can accomplish a great deal in his/her first year, he/she needs to be sensitive to the pace and timing of his/her activities. It is critical to be there when good things happen to sing people's praises. It is also critical to be there when things do not go well to own at least some of the responsibility and to do problem-solving.
6. Start small and go slowly. Develop relationships with subordinates. The superintendent can build trust with subordinates by learning about them and demonstrating he/she values their work. The superintendent needs to be thorough in his/her approach to implementing new ideas and new ways of doing things. Even when the ideas are good and staff believe the change would improve the organization, moving to implement change too dramatically and too quickly kills both the ideas and, ultimately, support for the superintendent.

Finally, the superintendent needs to act in trustworthy ways: open, honest, sincere, and dependable. Once people know he/she "walks his/her talk," future issues can be addressed in a spirit of trust and understanding.

Scenario:
The board voted 4–3 to dismiss its current superintendent. As a result, it agreed to hire a professional search firm to assist with the hiring of a new superintendent. The board spent several weeks conducting an open forum to receive input from students, teachers, parents, and community members about what was working in the district and what was not working. When the interview process produced three out-of-district finalists, the board invited the top three finalists to the community for a public "meet and greet." Following the feedback from the "meet and greet," the board agreed at its next public board meeting to recommend and vote on a superintendent finalist. After much discussion at the board meeting, a motion to hire a finalist and a second were made. The board voted 4–3 to hire the recommended finalist. The board president notified the finalist who was approved by a 4–3 board vote. When the finalist learned that she was approved by a split vote, she declined the board president's offer stating that she was uncomfortable starting a highly complex and demanding job without the full support of the board.

Questions:

1. What could the board have done differently throughout the process to ensure a successful outcome?
2. If the board knew that its vote to approve the new superintendent was not unanimous, what should the board have done differently to avoid a 4–3 vote?

3. If you were a finalist for the position and offered the superintendent role, would you have accepted the position with the board producing a split vote? Why or why not?
4. How do you think the students, teachers, parents, and community members who were actively engaged in the interview process might react to the outcome?
5. If you were the finalist for the superintendent position and declined the board's job offer, what, if any, impact might you experience in your current community once it is learned that you were interviewed to leave the job you currently hold? How should you address the attention?

NOTES

1. National School Boards Association (2020). *How structured interviews help school boards make better superintendent selections.* Alexandria, VA: NSBA Publication.

2. National Policy Board for Educational Administration (2015). *Professional standards for educational leaders.* Reston, VA: National Policy Board for Educational Administration.

3. Judge, Timothy, Higgins, Chad, and Cable, Daniel (2000). Employment Interview: A review of recent research and recommendations for future research. *Human Resource Management Review*, 10(4), pp. 383–406.

4. Recker, Leslie (2022). *How school boards choose a superintendent.* San Diego, CA: Ed100 Publishing.

5. Krosel, Amber, Eads, Audrey, Sherman, Cindy, and Gafner, Jocelyne (2023). *15 things you should do before an interview.* Indeed Career Guide. https://www.indeed.com/career-advice

6. Kerrins, Judith A. and Cushing, Katherine S. (2001). The classic mistakes of new superintendents. *School Administrator*, 158(2), pp. 38–41.

Chapter 3

Negotiating the Superintendent's Contract

"Everything you say should be true, but not everything true should be said."

Voltaire

Voltaire was a French Enlightenment writer, philosopher, satirist, and historian. Famous for his wit and his criticism of Christianity and slavery, Voltaire was one of the first authors to become renowned and commercially successful internationally.

Negotiating superintendent contracts is an important aspect of school administration. It involves establishing the terms and conditions of employment for superintendents and determining the superintendent's financial well-being. The contract

- sets the superintendent's salary.
- provides the superintendent with other financial benefits.
- determines the superintendent's financial stability in retirement.
- sets forth the parameters for expectations and the evaluation cycle.
- imposes legal obligations upon the superintendent and the school board.

A school superintendent can negotiate his/her own contract, but it is important to approach the negotiation process with care. Usually, the determination of whether the superintendent negotiates his/her own contract is whether the superintendent is negotiating with members of the school board or the board's legal representative. If the superintendent is negotiating a contract with the board's attorney, the superintendent should consider hiring an attorney to negotiate his/her contract because a board's attorney has ethical obligations to the board of education but has no such obligations to the superintendent.

As a result, counsel for the board will be interested in getting the "best deal" for the board, not for the superintendent.

The negotiation process can set the tone for the superintendent-board relationship. It is advisable for both parties to approach the negotiation collaboratively and aim for a win-win outcome. It is crucial to avoid starting the superintendent-board relationship on a bad note. Negotiating a superintendent contract requires a balance between the board protecting the interests of the school district and maintaining a positive working relationship with the superintendent. The superintendent must also be cognizant of the interests of the school district and be fiscally responsible in his/her negotiations. Most superintendents prefer a painless process and may be willing to make concessions.

According to attorney-at-law, Ashley Story,[1] the superintendent contract varies substantially with most contracts typically covering several core elements. These elements include term, duties and responsibilities, compensation, benefits, creative compensation ideas, indemnification clause, performance evaluation, termination, and buyout clause.

1. Term

The term of a contract is the length of time over which the contract will be valid. Most superintendent contracts are for a term of three years; however, a board may consider a different term based on the needs of the district or the needs of the superintendent. As the contract term approaches expiration, the board has the choice of whether to renew a superintendent's contract. Be aware that some contracts call for automatic renewal.

Sample of language addressing the term of the contract: "The board, in consideration of promises herein contained of the superintendent, hereby employs and the superintendent hereby accepts employment as superintendent of the district for a term commencing July 1, 2023, and ending June 30, 2026."

2. Duties and responsibilities

School superintendents hold a powerful and often difficult role in a community as they must be competent, experienced, and versed in all aspects of the school district. In addition to being charged with overseeing all district staff, they are chief executives, leading all financial and business operations. Consequently, the contract is the place for the board to set out its expectations and responsibilities of the superintendent.

Sample of language outlining expectations and responsibilities: "The superintendent shall have charge of the administration of the district under the direction of the board. He/she shall be the chief executive officer for the board; shall select, organize and assign all personnel, as best serves the district, subject to the approval of the board; shall oversee the instructional program and business affairs of the district; shall from time to time suggest regulations, rules, and procedures deemed necessary for the well ordering of the district; and in general perform all duties incident to the office of superintendent as prescribed by board policy and such other duties as may be prescribed by the board from time to time."

3. Compensation

The salary is the most visible figure in a contract and will receive the greatest amount of scrutiny as superintendent salaries are public information and local media often report on them. It is important that both the superintendent and the school board are comfortable with the amount and can sufficiently articulate why the salary is justified. Salary factors should include:

- market rates in comparable districts
- qualifications
- stage of career/experience
- cost of living differences
- past performance
- previous superintendent's compensation

Sample of language tied to compensation: "The board shall pay the superintendent an annual salary of Two Hundred Thousand and No/100 Dollars ($200,000.00). The annual salary rate shall be paid to the superintendent in accordance with the schedule of salary payments in effect for other certificated employees of the district. Further, the board and the superintendent may mutually agree to adjust the salary of the superintendent during the term of this contract, based on the results of an annual performance review, but in no event shall the superintendent be paid less than Two Hundred Thousand and No/100 Dollars ($200,000.00)."

4. Benefits

The superintendent's contract usually sets out all of the benefits of the job of the superintendent. Types of benefits that are typically set out in the contract include

- vacation and sick leave

Sample of language associated with vacation and sick leave: "The superintendent shall be entitled to all benefits of administrative employees of the district, including but not limited to sick leave, vacation leave, etc."

- tax-sheltered annuities

Sample of language associated with annuities: "The district shall make an annual contribution to an annuity plan of the superintendent's choice in the amount of 10 percent of the base salary, with the first such contribution being made on or before. . . ."

- health and life insurance provisions
- retirement programs (pension system and retirement plan contributions)

Some superintendent contracts provide non-traditional benefits such as:

- technological devices which may include a smartphone, laptop, and tablet.

Sample of language pertaining to technological devices: "The district will provide the superintendent with a smartphone, a laptop, and a tablet which the superintendent may use in the performance of his/her duties and for reasonable personal use."

- professional membership dues or community service organizations

Sample of language connected to professional membership dues: "The district shall pay the superintendent's dues to the American Association of School Administrators, the State Association of School Administrators, and any other professional group or community/service organization memberships that the superintendent believes are necessary to maintain and improve professional skills or community relations."

- automobile allowance

Sample of language to support an automobile allowance: "The board shall provide the superintendent with a monthly automobile use and maintenance allowance of One Thousand Dollars ($1,000) to cover expenses related to travel in and around the district."

5. Creative compensation ideas

Superintendent contracts have trended to include more creative compensation ideas particularly since salary can be a lightning rod in some communities. The board must use other types of compensation to attract or retain an experienced, successful superintendent. These ideas include:

- performance bonus
- payment of medical plan premiums
- payment of unused vacation/sick days
- employer paid supplemental retirement plan
- advanced degree stipend

- life insurance supplement
- guaranteed annual salary increase percentage
- expense allowance
- extra personal/vacation days
- professional development

6. Indemnification Clause

The superintendent contract should include an Indemnity Clause that protects the superintendent from any claims, torts, or suits brought against his/her role as superintendent during his/her tenure and upon separation from the district.

Sample of language related to the Indemnity Clause: "The district agrees that it shall defend, hold harmless, and indemnify the superintendent from any and all demands, claims, suits, actions, and legal proceedings brought against the superintendent in his/her individual capacity or in his/her official capacity as an agent/employee of the District, provided the incident or occurrence giving rise to the claim or action took place while the superintendent was acting within the scope of his/her employment and, provided the superintendent and the district do not have adverse interests in the matter."

7. Performance evaluation

One of the major ways to maximize the superintendent's performance is to conduct regular performance evaluations. This process gives board members the opportunity to honestly analyze the superintendent's progress in a variety of areas. It provides an effective avenue for communication between the board and superintendent about the superintendent's job performance. It can serve as a corrective measure and lead to positive results. Many boards mandate that performance evaluations take place on an annual basis in the superintendent's contract. Standard performance evaluations are conducted by board members filling out a scoring rubric. This rubric typically looks at a variety of "domains" including, but not limited to:

- policy and governance
- policy and assessment
- instructional leadership
- hiring and leadership development
- organizational development and management
- communications and community relations
- professionalism
- teacher negotiations

Once school board members grade the superintendent, their scores are added up and averaged among all board members to rate the superintendent's performance. Objective and subjective criteria are important. During the time that the school board evaluates the superintendent each year, the superintendent should also take the time to complete a self-evaluation. This process will essentially mirror the board's evaluation of the superintendent. The superintendent should grade himself/herself on the same criteria that the board used to evaluate him/her. This process will further facilitate a dialogue between the superintendent and the school board and assist the board in determining the superintendent's annual salary percentage increase.

Sample of language related to the superintendent's performance evaluation: "A formal performance evaluation shall be conducted by the board prior to December 15, 2023, and subsequently during the month of November for each succeeding year, unless rescheduled by mutual agreement of the superintendent and the board. The board also may conduct an informal interim performance evaluation of the superintendent prior to December 2023. Such interim review shall consist of a discussion between the board and the superintendent about his/her performance and shall not require the completion of a written evaluation instrument."

8. Termination

The language in the Termination for Cause section of the superintendent's contract needs to be clear and unambiguous. This section of the superintendent's contract is extremely important and should avoid unnecessary language that is subjective in nature. The five common contractual grounds for termination include:

- mutual agreement of the parties
- voluntary termination by the superintendent (compensation and benefits cease on the day of separation
- disability of the superintendent (illness or incapacity impacts the superintendent's ability to fulfill job obligations)
- discharge for cause (cause refers to criminal conduct, unprofessional conduct, neglect of duty, dishonesty, or significant incompetency)
- unilateral termination of the superintendent (requires a vote of the board and may include the payment of a severance package)

9. Buyout clause

This provision is one way a superintendent can gain job protection. As a result, more and more contracts for superintendents contain buyout clauses. The language in the Termination without Cause Section (Early Termination) should allow for a buyout and health benefits. In some states, superintendents are allowed up to a twelve-month buyout and health benefits during the same period of time.[2]

Sample of language connected to the Buyout Clause: "In the event that the board terminates the superintendent without just cause, the superintendent shall not be entitled to appear before the board; however, the district shall pay to the superintendent, upon the execution of a complete release satisfactory to the board, severance pay equivalent to one year's total compensation."

Over the years, superintendent contracts have become more complex. Their complex nature can make them confusing for some board members and new superintendents who are unfamiliar with executive compensation. The language contained in contracts is critical for both compensation and governance provisions. Superintendents should request enough time to review the contract. When establishing a deadline for the superintendent to sign his/her contract, the board should provide ample time for him/her to review the contract. The contract will govern the superintendent's relationship with the district, so time for review and assistance with the review is critical. Also, both parties should make sure the wording in the contract is clear, specific, and doesn't leave room for ambiguity. If necessary, superintendents should not hesitate to consult an attorney as legal representation can help to protect the parties from legal liability and assist in setting the tone for the superintendent-board relationship.

Scenario:
The superintendent's contract was due to expire on June 30, 2023. In January 2023, the school board unanimously voted to renew the superintendent's contract and extend it through June 30, 2027. In April 2023, after receiving proper written notification, a veteran administrator had his contract non-renewed for failing to address previously documented insufficient leadership practices including multiple years of well below-average student achievement. As a result of the veteran administrator's contract non-renewal, the board received multiple complaints from community members. The board held open community forums to allow community members' voices to be heard on the matter, but the forums were not well orchestrated, and they turned into unorganized grievance sessions which allowed community members to complain about anything and anyone related to the schools. Following the forums, the board decided to non-renew the superintendent's contract. Because the board failed to provide proper written notification of its decision not to re-employ the superintendent, the board voted by a simple majority to buy out the superintendent's contract. The cost to the board and local taxpayers was an expensive six-figure settlement.

Questions:
1. Was the board acting with good authority to dismiss the superintendent? Why or why not?

2. Should local taxpayers be concerned about a six-figure payout to get the superintendent to leave his position? Why or why not?
3. What steps might the superintendent have followed in an effort to avoid a confrontation with the board leading up to the contract non-renewal of the veteran administrator?
4. Does the superintendent have a case for "wrongful termination?" Why or why not?

NOTES

1. Story, Ashley (2023). *Closing the deal and getting real: Superintendent contract negotiations and evaluations.* Columbia, SC. White and Story LLC, Attorneys at Law, Columbia, S.C.

2. Association of California School Administrator (2023). *10 tips for superintendents signing their first contract.* Sacramento, CA. ACSA.

Chapter 4

Working to Develop Trust and Mutual Respect

"Trust takes years to build, seconds to break, and forever to repair."

Anonymous

Building effective superintendent-school board relationships is a continuous process. Whether a new or a seasoned veteran, the effective superintendent knows that building a solid board relationship takes priority. The position comes with endless high-priority tasks, of which the most essential is to build trust and mutual respect between the superintendent and the board. Trust and mutual respect are the bedrock of all successful relationships and the foundation upon which a culture of innovation and risk-taking supports continuous improvement. Superintendents who establish and build trust and mutual respect with board members are more likely to accomplish work toward meeting district goals, supporting student achievement, and creating the capacity to implement adopted strategies.[1] Although the relationships between the superintendent and the board may straddle the personal/professional line, board members understand that building trust and mutual respect are not the same thing as making friends. Establishing trust and mutual respect requires follow-through on promises, a demonstrated interest in and consideration of others' viewpoints, and honest and authentic communication. A lack of trust and mutual respect can quickly destroy the hard work being done by leadership team members. Negative behaviors by board members or superintendents can drastically reduce the opportunity for collaboration, ruining the opportunity for good governance.

According to Hackett,[2] there are several efforts that will assist the superintendent in becoming the type of leader who is worthy of trust and who leads a group of goal-minded leaders the superintendent can trust in return. Some of these efforts include:

1. Superintendents should establish regular times to check-in.

    This would include regular school board meetings that have a standing agenda item to discuss new business and topics the school board members wish to address. School board members are well-positioned to offer valuable insights into opportunities, trends, and potential issues that should be addressed by the collective leadership. By adhering to this format, superintendents can demonstrate to their school board members that they value the board's input, are open to the board's concerns, and genuinely want to discuss the topics that matter to the board. This process will help to develop a foundation for long-term trust and mutual respect.
2. Superintendents should work with their school board members to establish district goals.
3. It is believed that good leaders set goals for their team but great leaders collaborate with their teams to set goals together. Consequently, superintendents need to set aside time each year to decide as a collective group what the most critical area(s) of focus will be for the year and what steps need to be taken to achieve a successful outcome. According to the National School Boards Association,[3] effective school boards should establish a clear vision with high expectations for quality teaching and learning that supports strong student outcomes. Limit goals to three or four, not ten or eleven so that stakeholders know the highest priorities for the year.

    It is only natural when board members are part of the goal-setting process, and have their opinions and advice taken into consideration, they will be more likely to possess a sense of ownership over any identified action items needed for success. Additionally, when difficult decisions need to be made in school districts committed to positive change, the superintendent and school board will be making those difficult decisions and implementing important policy changes together.
4. Trust and mutual respect naturally develop from an environment in which both parties hold themselves and one another accountable.

    From individual meeting follow-ups and action items to large-scale district-wide program success, every assigned responsibility is an opportunity to prove accountability and generate trust.
5. Superintendents must complete their responsibilities and set clear expectations for what they need from the school board members, including a deadline.

    After establishing what is required, superintendents must hold school board members accountable for their assignments, action items, follow-ups, and overarching duties and responsibilities. By holding others to

the same standards that the superintendents hold themselves, they prove their trustworthiness and earn respect.
6. Superintendents should allow school board members to share their opinions and ideas before they share their own.
7. This demonstrates to school board members that the superintendent values the board's input and that their ideas can impact outcomes. After every school board member has an opportunity to be heard, the superintendent then can establish a resolution. By speaking last, the school board members will understand and respect that due to the superintendent's position, he/she has the final say as to how efforts will progress based on the school board members' input.
8. Superintendents should establish a practice of meeting with the board president to set the board agenda for the upcoming board meeting.
9. The board agenda and board packet should be sent to all board members prior to the board meeting to allow the board to review the agenda. By reviewing the board agenda, board members have an opportunity to ask questions or raise concerns prior to the meeting and be prepared for any discussion related to a board agenda item and not be surprised if issues or concerns are raised about agenda topics. Since board meetings are open to the public and often reported on by the media, this will reduce friction in the open meeting.
10. It may seem an obvious practice, but school board members will want to feel that they are prepared and always informed.
11. If school board members perceive that topics, issues, or items for a vote are presented to them unexpectedly and without an opportunity to prepare, it may raise feelings of mistrust and resentment.
12. The Center for Public Education[4] stated that school boards must "lead as a united team with the superintendent, each from their respective roles, with strong collaboration and mutual trust."
13. When apparent conflicts emerge between individual board members and the superintendent, the board president should play an intermediary role to help resolve those differences. When differences arise and issues intensify, school board members must trust that the superintendent will support them individually and collectively and can lead the resolution process. School board members want to know that if their actions or decisions are questioned by the media, business community, or the district staff, the superintendent will stand behind them and not redirect blame or responsibility. However, the inverse is true as well. The superintendent should expect the board to support him/her especially when carrying out the board's edicts.

14. Likewise, when the school district achieves success, communication outlets may turn to the superintendent as the advocate of the program or project.
15. This is a perfect opportunity for the superintendent to share with school board members and give them their public recognition and praise. The school board members will appreciate the acknowledgment, feel valued, and will trust the superintendent as a colleague.
16. When the superintendent demonstrates to school board members that he/she is open to feedback and values the school board members' suggestions and assessment of his/her performance, the superintendent allows school board members to trust his/her intentions and respect his/her role.
17. The Center for Public Education[5] determined that "effective school boards take part in team development and training, sometimes with their superintendent, to build knowledge, values, and commitments for improvement efforts." By participating in an annual superintendent evaluation with school board feedback, the superintendent exhibits his/her dedication to transparency, open dialogue, and collaboration.
18. When the school board chooses to conduct a self-evaluation, it is an indication of good governance. It makes a statement that the board of education is willing to reflect internally, evaluate its performance, and consider improvements. An annual self-evaluation is an important evolutionary step that the board must engage in to demonstrate that it takes its responsibilities seriously.

From the classroom to the boardroom, all levels of public education have (or should have) high expectations of shared accountability and engage in continuous improvement models which extends to the joint effort between the governance team—superintendent and the school board. Board self-evaluation tools help the governance team celebrate the board's strengths while identifying areas of improvement. According to Peetz,[6] an annual board self-evaluation

- helps boards identify where they are highly effective and where there is room for improvement.
- helps the governance team navigate contentious situations.
- provides governing boards and management teams with the tools to identify challenges early on and develop strategies to address those challenges in the interest of maximizing efficiency.
- unearths new issues to a board or may reveal the "elephant in the room" that everyone knows about, but ignores.
- refreshes the board's understanding of its roles and responsibilities.

- identifies important areas of board operation that need attention or improvement.
- defines the criteria for an effective and successful board.
- builds trust, respect, and communication among board members, the board president, and the superintendent.
- allows individual board members to assess their own contributions and work more effectively as a part of a team.

Successful boards and superintendents utilize an evaluation of their performance as a way to facilitate communication and remain focused on their purpose. The evaluation should be a facilitated process through an independent facilitator that allows every member equal participation, and the superintendent must be included. The evaluation tool should be oriented around standards, such as the NSBA Key Work of School Boards. The prompts within each standard should push board members to look for evidence supporting their ranking of board performance.

Board self-evaluations that are done well create an environment in which rich, forthright conversations can happen regarding how the board conducts itself, does its work, and leads the district. Many times, these conversations are challenging to have but are necessary for progress to happen. Board self-evaluation is all about improving communication. It is about working on relationships and understanding, even with those you may disagree with or not like.

Boards and superintendents that work together to maintain open and constructive communication about their roles and responsibilities create a leadership team that has a much greater opportunity to positively affect student and school outcomes. Effectual governance and school system management is a team effort and requires constant and regular assessment of both the board and its chief executive. This process leads to system and student improvement only if the board and superintendent develop a culture that prioritizes this as a critical element of delivering an excellent education.

The following is a sample of a school board evaluation which is utilized by the New York State Education Department.[7] The sample is just one of the five performance standards the NYSED employs with its boards of education. The NYSED states that the entire board should participate in the process from start to finish, and the board president or an assigned designee should be responsible for expediting the evaluation process. Evaluating the performance of the board is not the same as evaluating individual board performance. The purpose of the evaluation is to look at the board as a whole, although a side benefit may be that individual board members gain more insight into their roles and responsibilities.

Table 4.1 Performance Standards and Rating Scale

Professional Practice	Highly Effective (4)	Effective (3)	Developing (2)	Ineffective (1)	Possible Data Sources
	Continually exceeds the criteria	Consistently meets the criteria	Partially meets the criteria	Does not meet the criteria	
A. The board develops a collaborative relationship with the superintendent, keeping cooperation and respectful discussions at the core of its deliberation.					Communication policies or procedures
B. The board establishes effective communication with parents, students, staff, and community members while respecting the chain of command and lines of responsibility.					Schedules of or invitations to community forums
C. The board works with the superintendent to gain input from the community using forums, survey instruments, and other vehicles following agreed-upon procedures.					Reports or presentations on programs that demonstrate community partnerships
D. The board actively generates support for the district through its vision and promoting educational opportunities for all students.					Legislative meetings, letters, or advocacy effort

	HE - 4	E - 3	D - 2	I - 1	
E. The board is an advocate for the district's interests with legislators and other elected public officials.					Newsletters and website
Total = (Add Vertical Boxes)					Survey results
Average Rating for this Standard					
Comments					

Source: New York State Education Department (2015). Performance standards and rating scale. Albany, NY: NYSDE.

- Begin with a pre-assessment meeting among all board members to review and agree on the instrument, the process, and the evaluation timeline. Collectively, board members should review the standards of performance, as well as identify the annual board objectives based on the needs and priorities of the board.
- Determine if the evaluation process will occur only once, at the end of the school year as a summative (final) evaluation, or will also include a mid-year (informal) formative evaluation.
- It is recommended that each board member individually complete his/her own self-assessment instrument.
- The board president or designee collects all individual board member instruments and compiles the results and comments.
- Designate a special workshop session for team building with board members and the superintendent to discuss the evaluation results and provide an overall performance rating and a final comment summary with recommendations for improvement. At the same time, the board should define priority objectives for the upcoming year.

Performance Standards and Rating Scales: The five (5) standards of the board of education:

- Vision, Leadership & Accountability
- Board Governance & Policy
- Communication & Community Relations (Sample)
- Fiscal Resources, Staff Recruitment & Environment
- Ethical Leadership

Standard 3: Communication and Community Relations—The board of education effectively communicates with the superintendent and the local community, represents community interests and values, and ensures district information and decisions are communicated to the community.

The average tenure for a superintendent is approximately 2.5 years in urban school districts and 6.5 years in rural and suburban school districts. Therefore, some superintendents may not have the luxury of hoping a trusting and mutual relationship will organically develop with their school board members. Whatever the challenge, the superintendent needs to be genuine in his/her effort to earn the trust of their school board members and give them every opportunity to see and experience the superintendent's shared interests and desire for shared success. Furthermore, the superintendent should hold board members accountable and to the same high standard he/she holds for him/herself while stimulating a culture of transparency, collaboration, and open dialogue. These efforts will go a long way in creating a professional work environment where trust and mutual respect occur naturally between the superintendent and the school board.

Scenario:
Following a negotiation session between the school district and the teachers' union, the superintendent and chief financial officer provided an update regarding the progress of the negotiation process to the school board members in an executive session. At the conclusion of the update, board members were reminded that the information that was shared was confidential and was not to be shared with anyone outside of the room. The next day staff members were talking among themselves about the details of the previous day's negotiation session and reported that they received the information from two present school board members.

Questions:

1. Confidential information being shared in the public domain reaches the superintendent's desk. How should the superintendent handle this new knowledge?
2. Once the board receives notice that confidential information was leaked by a member of the board, how should the board address this matter?
3. Should the superintendent and full board meet to discuss this situation? Why or why not?
4. Should the board president be apprised and asked to intervene with the board members sharing confidential information? What information should be brought back to the full board for discussion?
5. If a meeting is held between the superintendent and board members, what might this meeting look like? What should be the outcome of this meeting?

NOTES

1. Dlott, Stephen (2007). *Surviving and thriving as a superintendent of schools.* Lanham, MD. Rowman & Littlefield Education.
2. Hackett, Julie L. (2015). *Building relationships, yielding results: How superintendents can work with school boards to create productive teams.* Cambridge, MA: Harvard Education Press.
3. National School Boards Association (2020). *How structured interviews help school boards make better superintendent selections.* Alexandria, VA: NSBA Publication.

4. Center for Public Education (2019). *Eight characteristics of effective school boards*. Alexandria, VA: NSBA Publication, pp. 11–12.

5. Center for Public Education (2019). *Eight characteristics of effective school boards*. Alexandria, VA: NSBA Publication, pp. 12–13.

6. Peetz, Caitlynn (2023). *Education Week*, Superintendent evaluations are murky, incomplete, unfocused. Here's why that matters. April 06.

7. New York State Education Department (2015). *Performance standards and rating scale*. Albany, NY: NYSDE.

Chapter 5

Establishing Clear Roles

"If your actions inspire others to dream more, learn more, do more, and become more, you are a leader."

John Quincy Adams

During his long diplomatic and political career, Adams served as an ambassador and a member of the United States Congress representing Massachusetts. He was the eldest son of John Adams and the sixth president of the United States, serving from 1825 to 1829.

Researchers widely acknowledge the importance of clearly defining duties and responsibilities among superintendents and school board members. Traditional conceptions of these two governing bodies hold that a board's domain lies in policy creation, while the responsibility of the superintendent and his/her administrative team is strictly policy implementation.[1] However, these roles have grown increasingly vague and diverse across districts in recent years. Superintendents are no longer simply tasked with school management; their duties have expanded into a variety of areas, including human resources, public relations, accountability, and student learning outcomes. Many cite this phenomenon as a shift in the traditional superintendency away from school management and toward "transformational leadership," an approach rooted in strategy and heavily focused on long-term student learning outcomes.[2] Simultaneously, school boards nationwide are venturing outside of their defined roles of strategy, leadership, and policy development, with many board members probing into administrative and day-to-day specifics, as well as advancing political motivations. The confusion and conflict caused by these blurred lines can prove detrimental to the relationship between the superintendent and school board members and ultimately the school district.

Role confusion between superintendents and school boards occurs when the two parties infringe on each other's responsibilities, causing tension. The most common type of role confusion in school districts involves superintendents focusing too heavily on policy and school boards extending too far into administrative functions. According to Caruso,[3] role confusion is often worsened by a single "lone ranger"—a board member who becomes unnecessarily involved in day-to-day operations and personnel issues by circumventing the superintendent's authority, meeting secretly with staff members, and applying inappropriate amounts of pressure on other board members and staff. Every experienced superintendent has stories about rogue board members, from those whose blustering adds hours to board meetings to those whose pandering is so deplorable that they mimic the questions that constituents text them during board meetings. This behavior can drastically reduce a board's ability to collaborate and effectively govern. A culture of trust and collaboration fosters best practices and effective processes that serve as a safeguard against those who grandstand and disrupt.

McCurdy[4] also identifies key behaviors that can cause or prevent role confusion, outlining the difference between board members who function as trustees and those who function as delegates. Fulfilling the trustee role, board members act rationally to serve broad public interests. On the other hand, those acting as delegates protect personal interests and the interests of factional special-interest groups supporting them. Trustees typically make independent judgments regarding a superintendent's policy recommendations, remaining as objective as possible. Their decisions ultimately demonstrate a concern for the entire community the district serves. However, delegates project political judgments onto the superintendent's recommendations. Often, unpredictable board members fluctuate between these two roles, depending on the issue at hand. Such motivations can lead board members to misunderstand their actual roles in the district.

Researchers have identified several other possible causes for role confusion between superintendents and school boards. Dawson and Quinn[5] argue that the governance process outlined in most boards' policy manuals causes role ambiguity. The traditional process of doing board business not only allows role confusion but also causes it. When both the superintendent and board share decision-making at the operational level, role confusion should not surprise anyone as confused roles are an inevitable by-product of such a process.

Role confusion, in part, can often be attributed to the expectations that many board members bring to their terms regarding a superintendent's performance and function. Board members often lack experience in school administration, leading them to perceive superintendent behavior through the lens of their own personal convictions. Among other sentiments, Kowalski[6] reports that board members often express the following opinions of their superintendent: that he/she lacks respect for board members; that he/she lacks integrity; that he/she fails to manage; that he/she is inaccessible; and that he/she fails to comply with community standards. By entering their terms with these preconceived notions, board members are likely to grow confrontational rather than collaborative, and ultimately attempt to micromanage and infringe on their superintendent's duties.

While collaboration and open dialogue are essential to establishing trust, creating lines of separation between board members' responsibilities and the superintendent's responsibilities is equally crucial. When entities come together to share accountability, both parties will be more willing to respect one another's roles. While school boards are typically elected by the community to identify and accomplish student goals, the position of the superintendent remains distinctly different. The role of the superintendent is to identify needs, establish policies, develop regulations, review staff effectiveness, provide leadership, and manage the district's daily operations. When school boards allow the superintendent to lead and when the superintendent enables school board members to influence policy, mutual trust and efficient operations come naturally.

Several general techniques and approaches may be used to avoid issues associated with role confusion. One solution involves holding school boards accountable for raising student achievement. Donald McAdams,[7] chairperson and founder of the Center for Reform of School Systems, argues that placing all the responsibility for raising student achievement with the superintendent is ineffective and sets the executive branch up for failure. Instead, board members are encouraged to set student achievement priorities and plan district structures to support the superintendent in reaching those goals. This form of collaboration keeps boards focused on strategy and also helps reduce superintendent turnover, a major inhibitor to district performance.

Scenario:
A newly elected school board majority believes they were voted into office by parents who were upset with the quality of teachers throughout the school district. After being sworn into office, the new school board majority voted to assign members of the school board to various district classrooms for the purpose of evaluating teachers.

Questions:

1. In your school district, are there clearly defined roles and responsibilities for the superintendent and board members? On a scale of 1–5 with (5) indicating successful implementation of roles and responsibilities and (1) indicating much more clarity of roles and responsibilities needs

to take place, please rate the success of executing the roles and responsibilities of the superintendent and board members.
2. From your observation, what do you perceive the roles and responsibilities of the parties to be?
3. Are the defined or observed roles and responsibilities of the superintendent and board members allowing for efficient operations and success of the district? Why or why not?
4. If role confusion exists in your district, can you describe where the breakdown is occurring?
5. Is there a problem with teacher evaluation? If so, what is the source of the problem with teacher evaluation? Does it begin at the top of the system, in teacher negotiations and the contract, or the principal's office? Finding the underlying issues should guide the pursuit of the fundamental problem of teacher quality issues in the district.

NOTES

1. Price, William (2001). Policy governance revisited. *School Administrator*, 58, pp. 46–48.

2. Thompson, Ray, Templeton, Nathan, and Ballenger, Julia (2013). School board presidents and superintendents' use of transformational leadership to improve student outcomes. *National Forum of Educational Administration and Supervision Journal*, 30(4), p. 1.

3. Caruso, Nicholas D. (2005). The lone ranger on the board. *School Administrator*, 62, pp. 8–9.

4. McCurdy, Jack (1992). *Building better board-administrator relations: A critical review evaluation of the significance of local school leadership and the board-superintendent relationship as a driving force behind it.* Arlington, VA: American Association of School Administrators.

5. Dawson, Linda and Quinn, Randy (2000). Clarifying board and superintendent roles. *American Association of School Administrators*, 57, p. 2.

6. Kowalski, Theodore J., McCord, Robert S., Petersen, George J., Young, I. Phillip, and Ellerson, Noelle M. (2011). *The American school superintendent: 2010 decennial study*. Lanham, MD: Rowman & Littlefield.

7. McAdams, Donald R. (2006). *What school boards can do*. New York: Teachers College Press.

Chapter 6

Building Communication Pathways

"The single biggest problem in communication is the illusion it has taken place."

George Benard Shaw

Shaw was an Irish playwright, critic, polemicist, and political activist. He wrote more than sixty plays with a range incorporating both contemporary satire and histerial allegory. Shaw became the leading dramatist of his generation, and in 1925 was awarded the Nobel Prize in Literature.

Like any relationship, the dynamic between the superintendent and school board members can be problematic. Poor communication often leads to difficulties and disagreements. A lack of clear and consistent communication can hinder any relationship, and this relationship is no exception. When it comes to school districts, superintendents may view themselves as the experts and consequently avoid sharing relevant information with and seeking input from board members. This can result in board members feeling alienated and can erode feelings of trust and respect. Further, board members often serve as community liaisons; thus, they need to be able to share accurate information and dispel rumors with community members as well as share community perspectives with the superintendent and district leadership. When board members are unable to articulate the shortcomings and attributes of the district, the community can lose faith in their efforts. Therefore, the superintendent needs to work with the board to identify protocols that promote effective and efficient communication, keeping in mind the size of the district, past practices, and culture as all contribute to expectations. However, what should drive the conversation is what works to help improve everyone's job performance. Consider setting a time to revisit the protocols as a team, to affirm what works, and address any issues or concerns.

According to the National School Boards Association,[1] communications between the superintendent and school board members must be timely, consistent, and focused on the needs and expectations of both parties. Whether the news is positive or concerning, the superintendent needs to inform board members as soon as possible. In between board meetings, the superintendent should utilize a dedicated channel to communicate with the board, such as directing communications through the board president, holding regular one-on-one meetings with each board member, or distributing weekly email updates to the board; however, bear in mind that any email sent to one or all board members is a matter of public record. It is important to treat all board members fairly and share information requests equally. For example, if one board member requests material about a specific program or school, send the requested material to all board members. Shared knowledge promotes collaboration, transparency, and trust.

School board elections often bring many challenges for superintendents. The introduction of new board members changes the composition, dynamics, and culture of the governance team. The initial period of unfamiliarity can cause tension between the superintendent and new board members and among old and new board members. Consequently, the superintendent and board will want to continue to:[2]

- Establish and maintain personal and professional relationships with one another by engaging in respectful and honest communication and demonstrating interest in consideration of others' points of view.
- Bear in mind that the Access to Public Records Act states that any material that is created, received, and/or maintained is considered a public record and can be inspected and copied, including most emails.
- Address issues before they become impossible to solve.
- Commit to consistently applying protocols that promote effective and inclusive two-way communication.
- Maintain a clear understanding of how each board member and the superintendent fulfill their respective roles and responsibilities and what support is required for one another.
- Ensure that the personal and professional relationships allow one another to recognize and support one another's political roles.
- Demonstrate to the public that collaborative relationships nurture honest discussion around the students' best interests and enhance decision-making.

Frustration and tension can be avoided through extensive board member onboarding and continuous improvement. Whether board members are elected or appointed, the astute superintendent carefully analyzes, builds, and nurtures a board member team focused on moving the district effectively and efficiently forward. This must be the centerpiece of the superintendent's daily work.

Onboarding—assisting and supporting in the development of skills, knowledge, attitudes, and so on, needed to be successful in the job of being a new school board member—is one of the best ways to head off potential conflict or division.

The marketing, public relations, and design firm, Creative Effective Lasting,[3] recommended that superintendents create a take-home single source of information onboarding binder for new school board members that would provide a payoff in goodwill. Each orientation binder would include items such as the following:

- A personalized welcome letter expressing excitement at the new school board member's upcoming service and a reminder of why everyone has accepted their role: the kids.
- The school district's mission, vision, and values.
- A list of current board members, their contact information, and a short bio on each. Knowing the board members beyond the boardroom is a great way to bridge gaps and develop trust.
- The leadership organizational chart that includes key district staff members.
- The list of board committees and appointments, the purpose or charge of each committee, and the individuals currently assigned to each.
- A calendar of upcoming meetings and any important dates board members should know.
- Any must-know legal information board members need including how open meeting laws work and other state-specific laws that affect board meetings. This information should be easy to digest.
- The district's communication plan, as it relates to school board members. Some school boards prefer to use social media and be in the public eye either as a unit or as individuals. Others prefer to work more quietly in the background. This is an appropriate time to orient new school board members to district traditions and expectations for communication as well as discuss transparency versus privacy laws.
- A list of school board policies and where to find them. The board policies should be easy to access and easy to search.
- An explanation of board roles. This varies significantly from school district to school district, and new board members may have gaps in understanding. Clearly delineate governance versus administrative roles and proactively help new board members to understand the difference. Onboarding is an opportunity to engage all board members in the discussion about best practices, roles, and activities.

Whether newly elected or incumbent, the superintendent needs school board members who are engaged, inspired, knowledgeable, prepared, and ready to work with the leadership team in order to be successful. Therefore, do not overlook the importance of helping new school board members transition to their role with school board onboarding.

Scenario:

The school board holds two public work sessions and spends three public board meetings discussing the following year's budget. At the superintendent's biweekly meeting with the board president to discuss the next board meeting's agenda items, it is agreed that the following year's budget will be added to the next public board meeting agenda. At the conclusion of the board's discussion of the following year's budget at its bimonthly board meeting, a motion is presented and approved to vote on the following year's budget. The budget agenda item failed to pass by a 3 to 2 vote.

Questions:

1. Given what little knowledge you have about the failure of the budget to be approved by the board, were the types of meetings held and the number of meetings appropriate for the topic? Why or why not?
2. Please list all the possibilities where the communication may have broken down which contributed to the failure of the board to pass the budget.
3. How could the board president and/or superintendent make certain that individual board members' priorities were articulated and considered for inclusion in the budget? If priorities were not considered or included, what process should be in place to address their exclusion?
4. What could the superintendent or board president have done to ensure the board's readiness to vote in favor of the following year's budget?
5. After a failed vote to pass the budget, what should be the next steps for the superintendent and the board?

NOTES

1. National School Boards Association (2020). *The key work of school boards.* Alexandria, VA: NSBA Publication.

2. Hanover Research (2020). *Effective superintendent & school board collaboration.* https://www.hanoverresearch.com/reports-and-briefs/

3. Creative Effective Lasting (2021). *School board onboarding in 3 simple steps.* Minneapolis, MN: CEL Marketing and PR Design.

Chapter 7

Realizing Ideologically Driven Politics

"Politics is the art of looking for trouble, finding it everywhere, diagnosing it incorrectly, and applying the wrong remedy."

Groucho Marx

Julius Henry "Groucho" Marx was an American comedian, actor, writer, and singer who performed in films and vaudeville on television, radio, and the stage. He was a master of quick wit and is considered one of America's greatest comedians.

The political nature of elected school boards is also commonly cited as a leading cause of role confusion. Under a traditional model, school boards function as an authority that benefits the community, with members functioning as statespersons who strive for objective, effective policy decisions. However, pressure from factional special interest groups and personal biases cause many individual board members to overstep the boundaries of their roles and attempt to intervene in administrative specifics. A national survey conducted by Michael Ford and Douglas Ihrke[1] found that a slight majority of school board members in the United States identified as liberal or conservative. Consequently, a substantial share of American school board members do hold clear ideological preferences. Ford and Ihrke also found signs of ideological diversity on boards, with 25.7 percent of respondents stating they shared political views with "few" or "none" of their fellow board members. So, despite being almost universally officially nonpartisan, school boards are not immune to ideologically driven politics. Under these circumstances, school boards are failing to act as a singular voice and serve the broad public interests while creating added tension in the relationship between the superintendent and school board members.

At one time, school boards were an afterthought of local government where concerned parents and community members volunteered their time to debate topics such as calendars, budgets, and textbooks. In recent years, the pandemic has brought new challenges to the superintendent and school board relationship and new topics such as equity, race, gender identity, and school safety; book banning have been presented at board meetings. Concerned parents and community members have attended school board meetings to raise apprehension and alarm about decreased in-person learning and increased remote learning driving a new era of political debates and school board recalls. Parents and community members are now viewing school board races as their opportunity to take back their school districts from a political agenda they oppose.

Traditionally, school board elections have been nonpartisan. However, with the current political landscape, political parties are emphasizing school board elections as a means of not only determining who the school board members will be but also shaping the direction of school districts. Programs, staff, students, and organizational continuity suffer when politics become a priority between and among board members and the superintendent. Conversations on education should include more discussions of effective school system leadership. Allowing misguided personal agendas to drive important conversations and taint relationships at a negative cost to students, staff, and the community is never good governance.

The superintendency is wrapped up in politics. The superintendent needs to remember that whatever he/she says or does to advance or oppose a board candidate will make its way to the candidate and the local newspapers. If the superintendent attempts to influence elections or appointments, he/she may experience the repercussions of his/her efforts. Over time, special interest groups may characterize the candidates the superintendent supports as "rubber stamps" and use these efforts to motivate the public to elect independent voices who associate opposition with independence.

Blumberg[2] says that changes in the superintendency over the last 100 years have less to do with substantive differences in the problems faced with boards of education and more to do with the changes in the politics of the positions. Superintendents have to be skilled at maintaining a balance among the various conflicting forces in the school community for this more diverse, open system to function effectively. Superintendents today often describe themselves in no-win positions, in which any significant decision they make may alienate and upset someone or some group. Unlike other visible public leaders, such as elected politicians, they do not have partisan coalitions to rely on for support in times of trouble. Also, unlike politicians, who cannot be easily removed from office until the next election, superintendents serve at the pleasure of the school board and can be removed at any time. To be an effective educational leader in the middle of this conflict and complexity, a superintendent today must indeed be an adept political leader—building coalitions and alliances among the various actors who have power in the school decision-making, negotiating effective compromises, and forcing and trading concessions when necessary.³

Scenario:
The school district considers itself a college preparation district as students are prepared and encouraged at a young age to enroll in Advanced Placement (AP) classes upon entering high school. However, at a recent board meeting approximately fifteen parents attended the meeting to speak during public comments and make a recommendation to the board to "do away with AP classes." The parents expressed concern that the AP classes do not provide racial equity as too few Black and Latino students are enrolled in AP classes. As a result, the parents want the AP classes eliminated and replaced with a one-size-fits-all approach that would give students of all races an equal education. When the parents completed their comments, a board member closely connected to the parent group made a motion to the board to vote on a recommendation to eliminate AP classes.

Questions:

1. What should be the board president's response to the parents? What should be the board president's response to the board member who made the motion?
2. What about this situation as it is described does not follow protocols or policies found in most school districts?
3. What one important group is missing from the conversation? What role should this group play in the discussion moving forward?
4. Who benefits from this decision? What is the replacement theory or practice being advocated here?
5. Regarding the topic brought before the board, what would be the appropriate next steps by the board and superintendent as it pertains to a few parents' recommendations for the elimination of AP classes?

NOTES

1. Ford, Michael and Ihrke, Douglas (2014). *Yes, school board members are often ideological, and that is OK*. Washington, DC: Brooking Institution.
2. Blumberg, Arthur and Blumberg, Phyllis (1985). *The school superintendent: Living with conflict*. New York: Teachers College Press.
3. Johnson, Susan Moore (1996). *Leading to change: The challenge of the new superintendency*. San Francisco: Jossey-Bass.

Chapter 8

Creating Strong Community Relations

"The public is the only critic whose opinion is worth anything at all."

Mark Twain

Samuel Langhorne Clemens, known by the pen name Mark Twain, was an American writer, humorist, and essayist. He was praised as the "greatest humorist the United States has produced," with some calling him the "father of American literature."

The number one complaint about school boards is they micromanage operational details that have little to do with student achievement. The cafeteria, bus routes, parking lots, athletics, and personnel assignments get far too much attention while the district's education program and the community's interests are ignored. Truth be told, a board will usually follow the superintendent's lead when it comes to establishing priorities, planning board meeting agendas, and communicating with staff and the community. The superintendents who fully understand the board's role help their boards represent community interests and stay focused on educational outcomes rather than sports, buses, and paint colors. The best way to keep board members out of problem-solving is to build a customer-friendly school district that responds quickly and effectively to parents and other constituents.

The superintendent and school board members must be a reliable conduit for two-way communications between the community and the school system. They must strive to increase community participation and support, but not ignore legitimate negative perceptions and pressure from constituents. Dawson and Quinn[1] state that cultivating business, civic, and community leaders, known as "key communicators," can be one of the most important and beneficial components of community outreach as it builds a focus on student achievement and support for district and board efforts. They can become knowledgeable about the school district and can serve as ambassadors. They can help head off misperceptions and rumors about school business and can explain the district's core beliefs.

As the saying goes, information is power. By providing first-hand knowledge of what is going on with the district and board, greater insight and understanding into the issues the district and board are wrestling with can assist in getting news out to the public and reduce the rumor mill among the school community. When people do not have enough information, they fill in the gaps. This is especially true if the organization is going through any type of change. When people encounter change, the first thing they try to do is figure out how it will affect them. With the recent growth in social media platforms in the last two decades, many school districts regardless of size have added communication specialists to build and maintain relationships with members of the community, key individuals, and other organizations; to respond to inquiries from community members; and to manage social media content and virtual groups to enhance the company's online profile. By being open and transparent, leaders can prevent speculation, gossip, and the spreading of rumors.

However, engaging with the public in a meaningful way has proven to be one of the most challenging and overwhelming tasks of many school boards. Without the superintendent's influence and persuasion, board members would not sit down with their constituents and engage in meaningful dialogue. Board members can use "key communicators" to inform their thinking, to leverage their influence, to build community understanding and support, and to help the superintendent and board demonstrate to constituents that it is in touch and cares about community opinion. Similarly, the gathering allows "key communicators" to hear the diversity of expectations among themselves and the challenges the board has in addressing complex and assorted public opinion.[2]

The "key communicators" group can consist of the mayor and some of the community's movers and shakers, but it should include parents and laypeople who are simply interested in learning more about the school district. Topics for discussion may include how school funding works, what it means financially for the district if an operating levy succeeds or fails, what athletics and extracurricular activities are not funded by taxpayer dollars, and what programs are unfunded mandates from the state and federal governments. It's an opportunity for visibility at schools and school events and a chance for parents and community members to meet in an informal setting such as a superintendent's breakfast and engage with constituents about what's on their minds. Finally, the "key communicators" group can serve as the foundation for a promising recruitment tool for new school board talent, especially as members begin to feel more invested in the school district's goals and become aware of the challenges it faces.

Scenario:

The school board of a school district in a small town has been facing a community relations problem. The problem started when the school board decided to cut funding for the school's music program. This decision was met with strong opposition from the community, especially from parents and students who were passionate about music. The school board did not communicate the reasons for the decision effectively, which led to a lot of confusion and frustration among the community members. To address this issue, the school board decided to hold a town hall meeting to discuss the decision and its implications. The meeting was attended by the school board members, the superintendent, teachers, parents, and students. The school board members explained the reasons for the decision and the challenges they were facing in terms of budget constraints. They also listened to the concerns of the community members and answered their questions.

Questions:

1. Was the town hall meeting held by the school board sufficient to rebuild trust with the community? Why or why not?
2. What, if anything, could the school board do moving forward to address community concerns?
3. What steps could the board undertake to improve its communication with the community?
4. How important is community relations for a school district? Should the school district consider creating a community specialist position? Why or why not?

NOTES

1. Dawson, Linda and Quinn, Randy (2019). *The art of governing coherently: Mastering the implementation of coherent governance and policy governance.* Lanham, MD: Rowan & Littlefield.
2. Dawson, Linda and Quinn, Randy (2000). Clarifying board and superintendent roles. *American Association of School Administrators*, 57, p. 2.

Chapter 9

Addressing Dysfunctional Leadership

"Last year we said, 'Things can't go on like this,' and they didn't, they got worse."

Will Rogers

Rogers was an American vaudeville performer, actor, and humorous social commentator. He was born as a citizen of the Cherokee Nation in the Indian Territory (now part of Oklahoma) and is known as "Oklahoma's Favorite Son." By the mid-1930s, Rogers was hugely popular in the United States for his leading political wit and was the highest paid of Hollywood film stars.

Lack of leadership is a frequently discussed topic in many school districts. While the conversation can focus on administrators and teachers, the topic seems to surface most frequently when people talk about school board members. An indicator of a problem is thinking and believing that one's election to the school board qualifies one to lead. Unfortunately, leadership is not the result of electoral success.

Leading a school district requires far more than knowledge and expertise. It calls for clarity of purpose, foresight and vision, and a commitment to collegiality, reflection, perseverance, and a deep understanding of policy and educational practice. It also demands a great deal of political insight, a decent dose of humility, and a phenomenal amount of courage.[1]

All too often, school boards spend a fair amount of public dollars conducting a search for a new superintendent to lead their school district. After months of recruiting and interviewing, the school board announces the hiring of a superintendent and declares that the new superintendent is a "perfect-fit" for the important work that needs to be addressed in the district. Unfortunately, the research shows that in far too many cases within a three-year window and despite the successes the superintendent may have experienced, the board is providing the superintendent with a separation agreement and beginning the search process for a new leader all over again.

American taxpayers trust more than $660 billion (about $2,000 per person in the United States) in spending to K–12 public education annually. While national education reform dominates media coverage, local school boards exercise considerable influence over student performance. Board members are tasked with solving important challenges such as aging facilities, budget shortfalls, and maintaining a quality and experienced teaching force while confronting and reducing achievement gaps. However, the difference between effective and ineffective school governance is clear among the approximately 13,588 public school districts nationwide.

Ineffective governance is often the by-product of what has been called "school board dysfunction," the situation in which board members lacking in organization, leadership, and an understanding of their role diminishes a board's capacity for good decision-making and strong educational leadership.

While a potential board member campaigning for elected office independently calls the shots in the campaign, the role of elected board members demands collaboration, a willing exchange of ideas, and acceptance of the school system's framework for advocating change as he/she is merely one of many in the decision-making process. When these practices of good governance are not upheld early on, relationships within the board and with the superintendent become tense. This is the beginning of dysfunction. This is the time that decisions and processes get off kilter. This is why

- board members navigating challenging and conflicting demands of accountability can lead to power struggles over decision-making.
- board members hire multiple superintendents in a short time frame.
- board members have differences of opinions on a shared vision when prioritizing a sports program rather than focusing on the broader, long-term efforts at improving student performance or civic engagement, or career and technical education.
- board members are influenced by personal agendas and give precedence to self-preservation or the desire to keep their elected position and avoid making unpopular but necessary changes.
- superintendents who meet or exceed the expectations set by their school board members will be asked to leave shortly after newly elected board members are seated in office.

Addressing dysfunctional leadership can be challenging but is crucial for the health and success of an organization. Here are some strategies to consider:

- Provide leadership development training for board members and include important elements of leadership in the new board member onboarding process.
- Foster an environment where open and honest communication is encouraged and practiced.
- Identify the issues and behaviors contributing to the dysfunction.
- Define roles, responsibilities, and expectations for leaders in an effort to work toward common goals.
- Conduct crucial conversations and address toxic behaviors directly.
- Establish a support network in the organization to assist board members in navigating challenges.

Putting these strategies in place will not only address dysfunctional leadership but also assist the superintendent in preparing and engaging board members in the important work of leading a school district.

Scenario:
In executive session with board members, the superintendent and legal counsel share the details of a serious personnel matter involving a well-liked teacher/coach. At the conclusion of the update, the board is notified that the teacher/coach will be suspended with pay pending the outcome of an investigation. The board members are told that if the charges are proven to be true that teacher/coach will be recommended for dismissal. Several board members asked the superintendent if he could "take care of this matter" so the board would not have to vote on the possible dismissal of the well-liked teacher/coach.

Questions:

1. Is there a leadership void at the superintendent or board member level? If so, what can be done to address the void?
2. Is there a good working relationship between the superintendent and the board? What accounts for the relationship being good or poor?
3. How many superintendents have served the school district in the last ten years? What do you account for so few or so many?
4. As superintendent, how would you respond to the board member's request to "take care of this matter?"
5. What has been the pattern of how your district deals with controversy?

NOTE

1. Martin-Kniep, Giselle O. (2012). *Neuroscience of engagement and SCARF: Why they matter to schools.* https://lciltd.org/WebsitePublications/Handbook Neuroleadership EngagementArticleGMK.pdf

Chapter 10

Partnering during Teacher Contract Negotiations

"We cannot negotiate with those who say what's mine is mine and what's yours is negotiable."

John F. Kennedy

American politician who served as the thirty-fifth president of the United States from 1961 until his assassination in 1963. He was the youngest person to assume the presidency by election and the youngest president at the end of his tenure.

The result of each local contract negotiation can vary in accordance with the skill, attitude, ability, and preparation of both the teachers' union and board of education's representatives, which includes the superintendent. Unfortunately, in most school districts contract negotiations create a relationship between the two parties that is adversarial and unpleasant. However, one important step to consider prior to the need to discuss an amended or new teacher contract is the implementation of a superintendent-teacher association team that meets monthly. The purpose of these meetings is to engage in in-depth conversations with teacher leadership and demonstrate an ongoing willingness to listen and receive feedback about what is working and what isn't working in schools or around the district. The outcome of these meetings usually reduces tension leading to contract negotiations and many times can resolve issues before they create adversarial positions.

Traditional or adversarial bargaining usually begins with each side staking out its position and making tough or unreasonable demands. In this "win-lose" negotiating environment, the party that is the most aggressive usually achieves an agreement that serves its interest and leaves the other party feeling frustrated and bitter. The impact of such conflict on a school system, particularly between district employees and the superintendent and board of education, can be a permanently damaging and divisive experience.

As a member of the district's negotiation team and working cooperatively with the board, the superintendent should strive to make sure all parties have their needs met in an agreement. The superintendent and board should value strengthening, establishing, and building relationships without compromising the district's best interests. This type of "win-win" negotiation is sometimes called collaborative or interest-based bargaining. This bargaining approach is where negotiating parties attempt to reach a mutually beneficial solution, invite parties to focus on finding mutually beneficial outcomes, and separate emotion from issues whereby parties can reduce emotional responses and personality conflicts by focusing on the issues rather than how these problems make them feel. The outcome results in students experiencing a better school environment; the employees having an improved work environment; and the community attitude remaining at the status quo stage or improving in support of the school district.

While all negotiations are not without their challenges, the following are some thoughts by Dlott[1] to consider as the superintendent serves as the catalyst for keeping the process moving forward.

- Employ a third party to facilitate the collaborative bargaining process. The process includes protocols that seek to get every voice in the room and build consensus for all discussable issues. The facilitator, more times than not, has experience with working in other communities around the state and can provide a perspective on other settlements and a sense of fairness.
- Review and provide an opinion on the reasonableness of the teacher and school board proposals. With teachers and school board members usually preparing for negotiation sessions with unreal expectations, the superintendent and chief financial officer should evaluate both proposals and the district's financial standing and make recommendations to the school board. The teachers' negotiating team meets with staff to establish what issues are most important to them. The result is usually a very long list of items that include current concerns as well as expectations to make up for salary agreements from prior contracts for which teachers were not pleased. The board's list of items usually includes the two most costly items for the board: salary and benefits. Hopefully, the school board will not develop a proposal without the participation of the superintendent and key members of his/her executive team.
- Present and accept all teacher demands. All too often, the teachers' negotiating team accepts and presents all teacher demands rather than saying no to any of their colleagues. There is no need to worry about the length of

the teachers' demands as dollar amounts are assigned to each demand in the collaborative bargaining model. Consequently, team members quickly learn the dollar amounts associated with the teachers' demands as well as the overall cost of the teachers' package. Most often, the teacher package is too expensive and unaffordable for the board; thus, priorities need to be discussed and identified to reach a reasonable resolution.

- Prove to be fiscally responsible. Ideally, the superintendent and school board have planned ahead, sometimes years in advance, to seek a mill levy to support the fiscal needs of the school district. However, in many cases, school boards nationwide confront public pressure to keep the growth of the district's budget to a minimum, including keeping teacher salary raises as moderate as possible. As elected officials, some board members feel a need to demonstrate to their constituents and other elected officials they are good stewards of the taxpayers' dollars and prudent in holding the line on budget increases.
- Refuse to accept the superintendent's advice. School board members have been known to reject the advice of the superintendent during negotiations. Some board members may view the superintendent as "one of the educators" and believe him/her to be soft when it comes to negotiations. Playing hardball, drawing out the bargaining process, creating adversarial relationships, and having the staff feel unappreciated during and after the negotiation process are not in the best interest of the board or superintendent.
- Recognize that teachers have advantages. School board members and the superintendent should recognize that teachers have advantages and strategies that can pose a challenge to the board and serve as leverage for teachers. As a rule, parents often support the teachers as these are the very people who are serving their children. Also, teachers can make the negotiations highly visible and portray the board and superintendent as unfair or heavy-handed thus applying pressure to reach a settlement sooner rather than later.
- Set ground rules. When establishing ground rules for bargaining with the teachers' negotiation team, a provision should be included limiting statements to the press and identifying only one member from each team who will speak to the press. Negotiating is an emotional process and inflammatory remarks to the press may fire up the community and teachers and make achieving a resolution more difficult.

Therefore, the most desired bargaining approach that leaves the parties with a healthy work environment and provides for continuous discussions regarding ongoing differences or complaints is to implement a collaborative or interest-based bargaining model.

Scenario:

After one of the negotiation sessions, a well-respected veteran teacher who usually spoke her mind visited the superintendent in his office. The teacher began the conversation by stating that "the school board offer was not fair." The superintendent repeated to the teacher what the board's position had been from the beginning of negotiations, "the economy is trending downward, and this state is not doing its part to adequately fund the public schools." The teacher said, "every time we head into negotiations, the school board says it is another fiscally challenging year." The teacher further stated that "even when the economy is prospering it seems every effort is made to limit salary increases. Teachers are having a difficult time trusting the board." The superintendent commented that "teacher salaries make-up 80-85% of the school budget and the board faces a great deal of pressure to present to the taxpayers a collective bargaining agreement that is considered reasonable." It has been publicly reported that dollars are available to grant a salary increase for teachers, but the percentage increase has not been shared or determined.

Although all team members are provided training on collaborative bargaining (win-win results) before the negotiation sessions begin, one board member who often prepares for bargaining with unreal expectations and rarely accepts the advice of the superintendent volunteered to serve on the management's bargaining team.

Questions:

1. If the school board is going to allow board members to serve on the management's bargaining team, how should the board determine which member(s) will serve? Should the superintendent have a voice in the process? Why or why not?
2. From the superintendent's perspective, what are the challenges with having board members serve on a bargaining team? What are the benefits of having board members serve on a bargaining team?
3. Should the superintendent share with the school board the comments presented to him by the well-respected veteran teacher? Why or why not?
4. What can the superintendent do to assist in setting reasonable expectations for collective bargaining with the board? What can the superintendent do to assist in setting reasonable expectations for collective bargaining with the teachers? What can the superintendent do to assist in setting reasonable expectations for collective bargaining with the community?

5. If your district does not have a superintendent-teacher association team that meets regularly to engage in in-depth conversations with teacher leadership, would you create one? Why or why not?

NOTE

1. Dlott, Stephen (2007). *Surviving and thriving as a superintendent of schools.* Lanham, MD: Rowman & Littlefield Education.

Chapter 11

Addressing Conflict/Power Struggles

"The harder the conflict, the more glorious the triumph."

Thomas Paine

Paine was an English-born American Founding Father, inventor, and political philosopher. He authored *Common Sense* and *The American Crisis*, two of the most influential pamphlets at the start of the American Revolution, and helped to inspire the colonial patriots to declare independence from Great Britain.

The school board is the superintendent's supervisor. The board represents the community, and the board should never be ignored, patronized, or treated as silent partners. Board members did not run for elected office to become yes-women and yes-men for the superintendent. Rather, they are civic-minded people who run for the school board for many different reasons. As superintendent, it is imperative that he/she values the board members' input and works in partnership with the members of the school board.

The superintendent should, however, never compromise his/her professionalism or integrity as these qualities are a necessity for success as a superintendent. Just as a superintendent needs the school board, the school board needs the superintendent. The superintendent has the expertise and the experience to deal with the complex issues that regularly face the school system. A superintendent does this daily, and that is what helps make the school system successful. School boards do want a capable decision-maker in charge as the school board is legitimately concerned about the welfare of the students. No school board enjoys seeing the system struggle due to poor leadership. The school board members rely on the superintendent to provide them with extensive backup material and information for their public discussions and well-thought-out recommendations, that lead to better decisions.

School board members want their input heard and considered. This does not mean the superintendent should ignore his/her own standards by merely doing things the board's way. A superintendent must recommend to the school board what he/she believes is best for the students, the staff, and the larger community interests. Although disagreements may occur with board members, reasonable people can disagree. The superintendent should be honest and straightforward about what he/she stands for and hope that it is respected. At the same time, being flexible enough to work with the school board if they choose to head in a different direction is equally important. Understanding the politics of the role of the superintendent is essential.[1]

In addition to working with the entire school board, the superintendent must address differences between individual board members to keep the board functioning effectively. Splits on the board can create hard feelings and can make the school board less focused and functional.

Scenario:

In one school district teachers chose to adhere strictly to their minimum required contract obligations (work-to-rule) if negotiations with teachers did not yield an agreement prior to the expiration of an existing contract. As a means of putting pressure on the school board, union leaders advised the board and the public that teachers would perform only required duties. The school board and the union often disagreed about which responsibilities were a regular part of the teacher's job. On this occasion "back-to-school nights" became the battleground. The teachers' union held that these evenings were voluntary meetings and that teachers would not attend. The majority of school board members were adamant that the back-to-school nights be held and that some punitive action be taken against absent teachers. The board planned to meet in closed session to make its final decision, and it was clear that most of the board wanted to force the issue. The school board conducted negotiations in this district and the superintendent was not an active driver of the process. If the superintendent adopted a passive, accepting role, it was likely there would be a destruction of trust between parents and teachers if parents arrived for the evening meetings that teachers refused to attend.

Questions:

1. Should the superintendent seek an opportunity to express his/her views and recommendations before the vote of the school board on this matter? If not, why not? If yes, what should the superintendent recommend?

2. If the superintendent's recommendation led to some school board members changing their votes to avoid a public battle between the teachers and the school board, would the resolution be considered a win-win, win-lose, or lose-lose resolution? Why?
3. The superintendent's intervening with the school board in this dispute can come with a price. What are some possible consequences the superintendent may face with his/her school board members moving forward?
4. After reflecting on the disagreement between the school board and the teachers' union, what are some ways this dispute could have been avoided altogether?

NOTE

1. Dlott, Stephen (2007). *Surviving and thriving as a superintendent of schools.* Lanham, MD: Rowman & Littlefield Education.

Chapter 12

Dealing with the Media

"Never pick a fight with people who buy ink by the barrel."

Mark Twain

American writer, humorist, entrepreneur, publisher, and lecturer. Twain was praised as the greatest humorist in the United States. He was known by many as the "father of American literature."

Historically, superintendents have been ambivalent toward journalists believing that many of them were only interested in negative news. In the present information-based society, however, enlightened superintendents realize that the media can perform some valued services, such as keeping the public informed of existing and emerging education needs.

Few professions require the rapid-fire and nerve-wracking pace of decision-making as the superintendency. The emotional nature of the issues that the superintendent confronts guarantees a steady diet of stress. Unlike a manager of a major corporation like the Ford Motor Company, whose goal is to capture only a share of consumers in the car market, superintendents try to please everyone, as even one disgruntled parent can create enough controversy to put the superintendent on the front page of the daily newspaper.

In most communities, local media covers public education continuously, and journalists' reports can be positive, neutral, or negative. Consequently, superintendents develop opinions that prompt them to view the media as an asset or liability. In his study, Kowalski[1] stated that just over half of the respondents (54.1 percent) viewed the media as a major or minor asset. However, superintendents employed in the largest districts (i.e., 25,000 or more pupils) were three times as likely to view the media as a major or minor liability than their peers in the smallest districts (i.e., less than 300 pupils). The difference between the two groups is logically explained by the fact that very large school districts receive substantially more media coverage and typically must deal with more social, political, and economic challenges and pressures.

The modern superintendent is expected to exchange information using print, broadcast, and social media. This requires an understanding of journalism, a willingness to develop positive relationships with reporters, an understanding of how to deal with negative news, the capacity to get the school district's messages before the public, and the competence to manage crisis situations (Kowalski, 2004).

Superintendents need to know what is newsworthy about their school district's activities and events and work with the media to maximize coverage. It's an age when people have incredible access to information. The media provides information 24/7 through television, radio, print media, and the Internet. Whether superintendents are attempting to provide a positive image to the public or dealing with a crisis, one of the most effective keys of sharing fast-breaking information with the public is to tap into this information stream. One way to implement this practice is to begin board meetings with a media campaign and showcase a school or a program that illustrates how the district is moving toward its aspirations and goals which are embedded in the vision, purpose, and principles that guide decision-making at all levels of the system.

As expressed by Blackburn and Williamson,[2] it's important to consider several key points for handling the media:

1. Identify media outlets. In order to successfully use the media, the superintendent must first understand the types of media available to him/her. Success will depend on a media list that must be continually updated.
2. Determine key people. The superintendent needs to determine the specific personnel who are important and with whom he/she plans to collaborate.
3. Build relationships. The superintendent needs to take the time to develop a positive strategic relationship with media personnel. There are several essential actions he/she can take to develop a relationship with key people. First, establish a repeatable pattern that integrates with appropriate social platforms to engage the media. This increases the superintendent's visibility and positions him/her as a resource and potential source of information. Next, develop a specific process so media personnel will take the superintendent's calls and meet in person. Maximize an in-person media visit or phone call. Go above and beyond the usual expectations. Finally, regular contact is always a plus in relationships. In subtle ways, keep in the forefront of all the media personnel with whom there will be interaction.

4. Conduct effective media interviews. The superintendent needs to improve his/her effectiveness when interviewing with the media. The superintendent wants to be certain that his/her message comes across. Additionally, keep in mind the following tips:
    - learn as much as possible about the reporter, the show, and the audience; be prepared
    - establish communication goals for each interview
    - redirect the interview to focus on key points
    - speak in memorable language
    - make certain the mind is in gear before the mouth travels
    - look at the reporter when answering questions; turn to the camera when delivering a key point
    - steady eyes suggest honesty; darting eyes suggest nervousness and dishonesty
    - anticipate questions and have answers ready
5. Develop a media team. The final key point is the selection of a media team or sub-committee. Due to the range of traditional media, as well as social media opportunities, it is unrealistic to ask one person to fulfill all the responsibilities unless the superintendent is able to hire a communication specialist. If a communication specialist cannot be hired, consider personnel resources and build on their strengths to develop the media team or sub-committee. However, be certain each member of the team understands his/her role, guidelines, and any limitations.

Traditional media is still a powerful advocacy tool. The superintendent needs to identify key media outlets, prepare for effective interviews, enhance his/her writing skills, develop his/her team, and utilize the media to get the appropriate message across.

Scenario:
Media coverage in the school district had been very limited. The reporters, one from the local paper and one from the radio station, regularly attended school board meetings. The media outlets that employed them usually reported the next day what they viewed as the key topics from the evening's meeting. The district and the individual schools produced quarterly newsletters and the district had a Web page that contained basic information about the school board and the individual schools.

After accumulating the facts about communication between the district and the stakeholders, the new superintendent prepared a brief report, which included a communication plan developed by her and the building principals. The superintendent forwarded the report to the school board members and thought the board would be surprised to learn what little communication had been taking place and they would have welcomed a proposal for a communication plan. Unfortunately, the board was not surprised or concerned. Summarizing the overall sentiment of the school board, the board president stated, "If the residents wanted more information about the district and the schools, they would have let us know." Also, after speaking with several board members the board president expressed doubt about the need for a communication plan and would table the matter if brought to the board for discussion. The superintendent explained to the board members that new outcome-based assessments mandated by the state required district resident involvement in school-improvement initiatives. Therefore, even if everyone were satisfied, the lack of stakeholder participation in visioning and planning would result in the district failing to meet the state mandate.

Questions:

1. Were the school district and the individual schools utilizing the local media to their benefit? If not, what could the district do to expand media coverage, especially in increasing stories that highlight effective programs?
2. If the school district has a positive image, are board members correct in suggesting that a communication plan is unnecessary?
3. Should the superintendent involve people other than the building principals in drafting and implementing a communication plan? Why or why not?
4. What options are available to the superintendent because of the board's decision to table the recommendation to approve a communication plan?
5. Should the superintendent share the perceptions he/she has gathered from staff and community members? If so, what might that look like?

NOTES

1. Kowalski, Theodore (2011). *Public relations in schools.* Upper Saddle River, NJ: Prentice Hall.
2. Blackburn, Barbara R. and Williamson, Ronald (2019). *5 Keys to handling the media for school leaders.* Washington, DC: edCircuit.

Chapter 13

Working with Standing Committees

"Coming together is a beginning, staying together is progress, and working together is success."

Henry Ford

As the founder of the Ford Motor Company, Ford is credited as a pioneer in making automobiles affordable for middle-class Americans through the system that came to be known as Fordism.

Structure is a key element of the board's governing design. Some aspects of the school board structure are typically inflexible, such as the size of the board or the frequency of its meetings. Many boards are looking for flexible ways of managing their workload. Adjusting to the board's evolving needs and standing committees seems to be a practical way to structure and manage the board's work. However, the use of standing committees is usually a matter of board discretion, and experience has taught that well-designed standing committees can make a powerful contribution to successful governing. Experience has also taught that a poorly designed committee structure can be a major impediment to the board's governing and is probably worse than having no standing committee at all.

Well-designed standing committees enable board members to divide the detailed work of governing, gain in-depth expertise in doing governing work, as well as provide a venue for intensive board-staff interaction that is not feasible at regular board meetings. Some key characteristics of well-designed standing committee structures as described by Eadie[1] that facilitate strong governance are the following:

- Standing committees that correspond to broad governing functions (i.e., planning or performance oversight) rather than narrow administrative functions (i.e., personnel or finance) or programmatic areas (i.e., instruction or athletics). Narrowly constituted committees can easily get more involved in administering than governing and feel invited to meddle in programmatic and administrative matters.
- Standing committee chairs comprise an executive or governance committee headed by the board president with the primary responsibility of ensuring that the board functions as an effective governing body.
- All board members serve on one and only one standing committee, apart from the executive or governing committee. This is the most important way to ensure in-depth attention to governance matters and avoid stretching board members too thinly.
- The superintendent assigns a member of his/her executive team to serve as the chief support person for, and liaison with, each of the standing committees.
- The only path to the full board agenda is through the standing committees, which are responsible for introducing all items and making all reports at regular board meetings.

Most school boards consider standing committees an essential part of their structure. Traditionally, the bylaws define the standing committees and the participants' roles. According to BoardSource,[2] in 1994, school boards had an average of 6.6 standing board committees while currently the average number of school board standing committees is 4.1. The most common standing board committees are finance, executive, fundraising, and governance. Sometimes a smaller group can be more focused and efficient in dealing with issues than the full board. However, it may mean that the superintendent will have additional people seeking his time to answer district level questions or discuss reasons for decisions that may have been board-driven. Any recommendations made by a standing committee need to be approved by the whole school board, but it is important to note that the board is not obligated to follow the standing committee's suggestions.

Scenario:
The State Department of Education mandated that all schools create a standing committee named the District Accountability Committee (DAC). The board provided a committee description that included a code of conduct. The committee description also included keywords or phrases such as "provide consultation," "make recommendations," and "advisory to the board." The board stated in its description of the DAC participants that "all membership will be appointed and approved by the board." The minimum number

of approved members to the DAC included four people: "a teacher, a parent, a taxpayer from the district, and a school administrator." Within a few days, a very assertive parent appointed herself the president of the DAC and began recruiting like-minded people to the committee. This group's agenda included targeting teachers and administrators with whom they had grudges and telling school and district administrators and the board what they needed to change. The school board president not only refused to confront this group and the fact that not one member had been approved by the board for membership on the DAC but also agreed to hear the "committee's" complaints and demands at public board meetings.

Questions:

1. What is the role of the superintendent in this matter?
2. If the board president refused to confront this situation, what recourse does a board member have?
3. Did the board president address this matter appropriately? If not, what were the mistakes the board president/board made?
4. What would have been a best-case scenario for addressing this situation?
5. What would have created a successful process for the unveiling of the purpose of the DAC and the board's expectations for the standing committee going forward?

NOTES

1. Eadie, Douglas C. (2003). *Eight keys to an extraordinary board-superintendent partnership.* Lanham, MD: Scarecrow Press.
2. BoardSource (2022). *Do we really need board committees?* Washington, DC: Leading with Intent.

Chapter 14

Balancing Work and Home Life

"Time is really the only capital that any human being has, and the only thing he can't afford to lose."

Thomas Edison

Edison developed many devices in fields such as electric power generation, sound recording, and motion pictures. He established the first industrial research laboratory and was one of the first inventors to apply the principles of organized science and teamwork to the process of invention.

Overwork is the new normal. Rest is something to do when the important things are done, but they are never done. Pang[1] dispels the myth that the harder we work the better the outcome. The author conducted research with an array of "workaholics" to challenge our tendency to see work and relaxation as opposing views. "Deliberate rest," as Pang refers to it, is the true key to productivity and will give us more energy, sharper ideas, and a better, more balanced life.

A certain amount of stress is present in any professional position. This is especially true in the superintendency, where the management of human and fiscal resources within a lay governance structure creates unique organizational conditions. Typically, superintendents seem to be on call twenty-four hours a day: pursuing additional education and professional development; attending meetings; going to athletic events, dances, concerts, community events, and churches; and participating in civic organizations. Besides district activities, superintendents often must attend regional and state meetings, visit the state capital and the legislature, and meet other superintendents throughout the area.

Unfortunately, time is not the only problem for superintendents. Devoted superintendents think about the job all the time. The job seldom leaves the superintendent's thoughts. This kind of commitment can cheat a superintendent of time with family, good health, and time for personal pursuits.

Therefore, superintendents need to spend time with family. Family moments and memories cannot be recreated or recovered later. The time spent with family needs to be quality time and if possible, the stresses and pressures of the job should be left at the office when at home. As important as it is to be a successful superintendent, these jobs will come and go. Your family should be with you forever. Make it a point to schedule time with your family/significant others/friends. Invest time in yourself and your health and give yourself permission to "rest."

Scenario:

The superintendent had not missed an end-of-the-year school-related activity since serving in the position for twelve years. This spring during the month of May the superintendent's only child was earning a Ph.D. and was graduating with honors. The superintendent planned with the school board to be absent for ten days to attend his child's graduation and travel with his spouse and child as a celebration. As a gesture of goodwill, the superintendent informed the inexperienced president of the teachers' association of his travels and the reasons supporting it. At no time during regular communication or preceding the conversation with the president of the teachers' association regarding the superintendent's upcoming travel plans did the president of the teachers' association share with the superintendent that any concern or problem was "brewing." The superintendent was six days into his travel plans when he received a message from his administrative assistant that the teachers' association at the high school conducted a "vote of no confidence" for the high school principal and shared the outcome of the vote with the local media.

Questions:

1. What, if anything, could the superintendent have done differently (or in addition) to prepare for or avoid an end-of-the-year crisis (vote of no confidence) at the high school?
2. What can you derive from the actions of the teachers' association regarding the process for the "vote of no confidence" and the inappropriate communication to the media?

3. How should the superintendent respond to the president of the teachers' association? The media? The board?
4. Should the superintendent cut short his travel plans and return to the school district to address this matter in person? Why or why not?

NOTE

1. Pang, Alex Soojung-Kim (2018). *Rest: Why you get more done when you work less.* New York, NY: Hatchette Book Group.

Chapter 15

Creating a Framework for Good Governance

"No man is good enough to govern another man without that other's consent."

Abraham Lincoln

Lincoln was an American lawyer, politician, and statesman who served as the sixteenth president of the United States from 1861 until his assassination in 1865. Lincoln led the Union through the American Civil War to defend the nation as a constitutional union and succeeded in abolishing slavery.

Governing is by definition the primary work of the school board, and one of the superintendent's chief responsibilities as CEO of the school district is to help the school board members accomplish governing work that makes a significant difference in the affairs of the district. This is the most direct path to board members experiencing the deep satisfaction that will help cement the superintendent's working relationship with the school board. Board members who aren't actively engaged in doing really important work tend, over time, to grow bored, frustrated, irritated, and often angry, making them difficult partners at best. Boards are magnets for high-achieving types who expect their work to produce important results, and nothing's surer to alienate them than feeling unproductive and underused.[1]

As the primary figures governing the local school district, each school board is entrusted with a great responsibility within their community. Implementing a school board governance model is one of the best ways boards can effectively and efficiently carry out their duties. It is important to note that school boards are designed to be governing boards, not management boards. Although school boards provide oversight in the superintendent's management, the school board's goal is to serve as reflective representatives of the public's interest. Despite having so much responsibility, school board members are often remarkably ill-prepared for service. About 40 percent of those currently in office have only three or fewer years of service and they are volunteers.[2] They run for office out of a general concern for the state of schools and the perceived need for change in current practices. However, once in office, they find the job demanding and complex. They are immersed in a set of financial and legal issues that few have the background to fully understand. They are expected to provide leadership when educational concepts are changing and complicated. Board members receive pressure from constituents that may lead them to make decisions for emotional or political reasons.

Unfortunately, few citizens are involved in the governance of public education with only 10 to 15 percent of the population casting votes in school board elections. One major problem faced by public school districts is that some members of boards of education attempt to exercise independent authority over superintendents, other district employees, and school district operations when individual board members have no legal authority. This condition creates tension between the superintendent and the board of education and has a negative impact on the school governance process. When boards of education and superintendents do not work together, the district suffers, educational quality deteriorates, and the community becomes frustrated and polarized. Without good governance, good schools are the exception, not the rule.

Critics say that school boards meddle in issues that should be left to professionals, treat schooling as a formal government program rather than a community-based caring function, and provide perches from which ambitious individuals can run for higher office. Members who micromanage, play politics, or intervene on behalf of individual parents or school employees do not misunderstand traditional school board roles; they understand them all too well.[3]

Given the difficult context within which boards function and the difficulty they have in focusing on their primary responsibilities, when school boards are unsuccessful, according to Smoley,[4] they often make the following mistakes in the way they operate.

- Making political decisions. School boards are in the business of making decisions. Unfortunately, boards often make decisions that are not based on objective information, assessment of alternatives, and rational judgment but have a partisan bias that supports hidden agendas and political alliances. When school boards conduct their business with partisan judgment, they compromise their capacity to govern in the best interest of children and the community.
- Functioning without a commitment to a district's stated purpose. School boards can fail to abide by or follow the core values approved for the district. Board members may drift toward their personal agendas rather than

toward the vision and goals established for directing their decision-making and work. Virtually every highly effective board governs with a unity of purpose driven by a shared moral imperative. These boards are highly engaged in supporting the work of the district.
- Functioning without ground rules. School boards often conduct their business without reaching agreement on the fundamental rules that guide their actions. Their failure to resolve some basic issues such as the roles of the superintendent and the board; the constraints on board members acting as individuals; the treatment of confidential information; and public decorum results in undermining trust and mutual respect.
- Responding to coercion. School boards allow particular constituencies to influence their decisions instead of making decisions that are in the best interest of all children.
- Failing to connect with the community. School boards may not provide information to the community, solicit input from the community, or fail to offer adequate opportunities for dialogue—all leading to community distrust and lack of understanding. Whether it's willful or out of neglect, when school boards do not fully connect with their communities they disregard a primary responsibility and seriously cripple their effectiveness.
- Neglecting self-improvement. School boards do not seek out self-improvement opportunities. Consequently, their performance is unpredictable and uneven. School board members feel the constraints of time and money and often decline training for self-improvement. Thus, the capacity for effective board leadership is not fully realized.
- Taking fragmented action. School boards experience problems when they consider each issue as a separate item rather than prioritizing based on the issue's contribution to overall objectives. The important school district direction is lost in conflicting or unrelated initiatives. School boards should form an effective "bridge" between the community and the school district—one that enables the district to understand the community's desires and needs and for the community to understand the district's work. School boards must build their capacity to govern with the superintendent and the community leaders contributing to this capacity building.

For most school boards, a traditional model is not a model at all. It is the absence of a model. Too often and for far too many boards, governance is a cobbled-together mix of practices based on tradition. There usually is no rhyme or reason why boards do what they do other than they have always done things that way. The boards' processes typically reflect the personalities and experiences of members currently serving on the board, along with those of the superintendent.

Even the best governance practices within the current model may be inadequate in the face of an education climate where the pace of change continually accelerates as its complexity grows. Similarly, as the size, scale, and scope of school districts grow, so does the complexity of the effective governance system, bringing increasing time and performance demands on superintendents, school boards, and their members.

Experts have been increasingly critical of school boards and their ability to function effectively. They see boards as unable to focus on policy, entangled in the details of personnel and student discipline, and unable to lead educational reform. If these actions weaken school districts and schools, some have suggested that school boards, and those whose educational leverage is acquired from a relationship with a school board (superintendent, district office staff, and teacher unions), need to operate as if they have one important job: making schools more effective through school governance.[5] The quality of governance that was sufficient to get school districts where they are today will be insufficient to get them where they will need to be tomorrow. The turning of generations, the changing culture, and a radically different economy have fundamentally changed the societal dynamics that gave birth to and sustained the traditional governance model. This model shows both its age and the early signs and symptoms of failure. Thus, some experts suggest changing to other forms of governance that provide the opportunity for greater policy focus.

One such form of school governance is coherent governance. It focuses school boards on their roles as board members of the school district they lead on behalf of the communities they serve. This board focus is centered on student achievement and how effective the school district is in producing results defined by the board.

Unfortunately, many school board members simply do not know what their jobs are. They busy themselves doing things, many times the wrong things, which results in frustration shared by everyone associated with the organization. It is important to recognize that in many instances these frustrations are due to school board members finding themselves entrenched in a governing system so inherently dysfunctional that failure is unavoidable.

A number of years ago Dawson and Quinn[6] conducted "exit interviews" with a number of retiring school board members. The authors asked the board members: "What prevented you from achieving all you had envisioned? What obstacles did you encounter?" Some responses were predictable: state and federal mandates, shortage of resources, union issues, and so on. However, what stood out was the number of times the authors heard responses indicating that the board's own internal operating systems and processes did not allow the board to do important work. Time was spent approving administrative recommendations related to operational issues and dealing with decisions that had been made long before the board meeting. Precious little time was spent on "kid issues" and too much time was spent on trivial matters.

Boards need to rely on a coherent system to get meaningful work done. According to Dawson and Quinn,[7] boards need a governing focus and a vision for what can be accomplished which includes:

- Board members need to address a few of their primary responsibilities in order to perform at a high level.
- Boards should focus on policy to drive important decisions.
- Boards need to document the percentage of time each board meeting is devoted to policy-level discussions. Truth be told, most boards spend almost as much time on operational matters as the superintendent does and the superintendent spends way too much time and energy in creating policy drafts for the board to consider.
- Boards need to document the percentage of time each board meeting is devoted to making policy-level decisions. Boards with the superintendent's guidance need to take the time to consider exactly what working at the policy level looks and feels like.
- Boards should resolve issues and provide organizational leadership at the policy level rather than deal with lower-level issues usually in a reactionary mode.
- Some boards believe it to be the role of the board to "manage the manager." The board may believe that it must check up on the superintendent and staff at every opportunity in order to assure itself that executive decisions are being made the way the board wants them to be made. Many superintendents are very capable of making some important decisions without the help of the board. The board is obligated to set the parameters for delegated decision-making. If the board cannot trust the superintendent to govern, although the board expressed confidence when it made the choice to hire the superintendent, then perhaps the choice should be reexamined.

Coherent governance supports the board by helping it focus on the organization's purpose and develop clear governing policies. From these new policies flow the organizational goals and the means to effectively measure results. It also helps the school board grapple with its critical relationship with the superintendent and the need to genuinely connect with the constituents of the organization.

Board members also must be clear about the purpose and function of the board as opposed to members' individual thoughts, opinions, and actions. This is very often where boards can go sideways as individuals try to press their own issues or want to be the star of the show. In coherent governance, the board is the star of the show.

The real value of using coherent governance is that it is based on principles that experts have long recognized as being characteristics of effective boards and a vehicle to enable boards to actually perform the way in which boards are intended to perform. In most organizations, good governance doesn't exist unless a board deliberately creates it. A coherent governance model based on fundamental principles and values can allow the board to build something greater than itself enabling board members to leave a legacy of visionary leadership for those members and staff leaders who follow.

Scenario:

A new board member joined the school board after low voter turnout in a relatively quiet election put her in the place of a two-term incumbent. At the time, people knew very little about the candidate (new board member). Later, she told the superintendent she had not expected to win, but won because the incumbent was "too lazy to campaign." Also, she stated that her interest was making sure her issues were important in the school district. Within a short time, the new board member set out to find a person in every school to give her any unfavorable information about the principal or someone on the staff. Her goal was to see the superintendent's reaction when she forwarded the negative information.

The superintendent recognized that these actions could not continue without substantial disruption to the organization. The superintendent also recognized that, as an elected official, this board member had some credibility in the community.

Questions:

1. What steps can the superintendent take in order to bring the new board member into the school system? What steps can the superintendent take to make the new board member a positive contributor?
2. What is the board's role in onboarding a new board member? What is the socialization process for adding new team members?
3. How can the superintendent help the new board member develop trust in the district and with the district's staff?
4. What might be the consequences for the superintendent and/or the district if the superintendent does not address the actions of a "rebel" board member?
5. How might an annual board retreat assist the board in its recommitment to the district's vision, purpose, and core values?

NOTES

1. Eadie, Douglas C. (2003). *Eight keys to an extraordinary board-superintendent partnership.* Lanham, MD: Scarecrow Press.
2. National Center for Educational Statistics. https://nces.ed.gov/fastfacts/
3. Boyd, William Lowe and Miretzky, Debra (2003). *American education governance on trial: Change and challenges.* Chicago, IL: University of Chicago Press.
4. Smoley, Eugene R. (1999). *Effective school boards: Strategies for improving board performance.* San Francisco, CA: Jossey-Bass Publishers.
5. Sergiovanni, Thomas J., Kelleher, Paul, McCarthy, Marthy M., and Wirt, Frederick M. (2004). *Educational governance and administration.* Boston, MA: Pearson Education, Inc.
6. Dawson, Linda and Quinn, Randy (2019). *Good governance is a choice: A way to re-create your board the right way.* Lanham, MD: Rowman & Littlefield Publishers.
7. Dawson, Linda and Quinn, Randy (2019). *Good governance is a choice: A way to re-create your board the right way.* Lanham, MD: Rowman & Littlefield Publishers.

Chapter 16

Utilizing Data-Driven Decision-Making

"In God we trust, all others bring data."

Edwards Deming

Educated as an electrical engineer, he developed the sampling techniques for the U.S. Census Bureau and the Bureau of Labor Statistics. He is also known as the father of the quality movement.

Today's school superintendents must wear many hats. They must have macro-level visions for their districts, set instructional goals, communicate constantly and repeat the mission with all stakeholders, manage employee relations, establish and maintain budgets, and take on challenges as they come. While working to achieve their district's goals, they make daily decisions that affect students, teachers, staff, parents, and the wider community. Because the superintendents' choices affect so many people, superintendents should implement data-driven decision-making in schools and create a culture of quality data that enables them to have confidence in the information they review and utilize to make effective decisions.

Data is also an essential component for school boards to make informed decisions. According to the National School Boards Association,[1] effective school boards are data-savvy and embrace and monitor data, even when the information is negative, and use it to drive continuous improvement. In addition, data can be used to measure student progress, evaluate program and instructional effectiveness, guide curriculum development and resource allocation, and promote accountability. Participants in continuous improvement processes must collect and use data to evaluate the efficacy of interventions, make midterm corrections, and plan future actions.

Consequently, there are four processes as expressed by Holmqvist and Ekstrom[2] that the superintendent and the school board can use to enhance the use of data for continuous improvement and to demonstrate compliance and accountability. The processes include:

- Data-driven insights. The first step is developing an understanding based on facts rather than assumptions. The superintendent should present data-driven insights about various aspects, such as student performance, staff performance, budget utilization, and school infrastructure to school board members. These insights help paint a comprehensive and accurate picture, setting a solid foundation for constructive dialogue.
- Transparency and accountability. The superintendent should ensure data is readily available and accessible to those who need it, promoting transparency. When school district leaders share this data with school board members, it fosters a sense of openness, responsibility, and accountability. Also, it assists in reducing confusion and possible misunderstandings, leading to more productive discussions and decisions. The data should also be readily accessible on school district websites.
- Ease of understanding. The superintendent should present data in visual forms like graphs, charts, and tables, making it easier for school board members to understand complex data. This visual data representation enables school board members to grasp key insights quickly, streamlining discussions and decisions.
- Trend prediction and future planning. The superintendent should provide information on the current state as well as predict future trends using algorithms and data patterns. This capability can significantly assist in communicating at school board meetings future plans and proposals backed by hard evidence.

According to the Center for Public Education's[3] study, board members in high-achieving districts identified specific student needs through data and justified decisions based on that data. In addition, board members were not shy about discussing trends on dropout rates, test scores, and student needs, with many seeking such information on a regular or monthly basis. By comparison, board members in low-achieving districts tended to greet data with a "blaming" perspective, describing teachers, students, and families as major causes for low performance. The study contrasts this with the policy of a high-performance district, where the superintendent "believes sharing information will get them to react and encourage engagement." Board members in this district view data as a diagnostic tool, without the emotional response of assessing blame. Board members in lower-performing districts also provided little evidence of considering data in the decision-making process. In these districts, board members frequently discussed their decisions through anecdotes and personal experiences rather than by citing data. In many cases, the study noted, the board talked very generally about test scores and relied on the interpretation made by the superintendent. As a result, board members believed the superintendent "owned" information, leaving it to the top administrator to interpret the data and recommend solutions.

Togneri and Anderson[4] also emphasized how effective school boards embraced data. Boards in high-achieving districts were not afraid to confront negative data and, in fact, used it as a basis to improve teaching and learning. Together, the board and superintendent developed goals and performance indicators to rank and monitor school progress. This process ultimately helped build trust among school and community leaders, eventually leading to district progress.

In summary, data plays a crucial role in the decision-making process of superintendents and school boards. It helps them to identify areas of improvement, align resources with district goals, and ensure that every child reaches his/her potential. The ability of the superintendent and school board to consider data in the decision-making process while focusing on student achievement is an important factor in attaining a high-performance school district.

Scenario:
The school board's agenda has a time designated for public comment. During this time, the public may register to share information with the board. At this particular board meeting, a respected community member who was upset with the standardized test results of an elementary school presented school performance data to the board. Unfortunately, the member of the public presenting the data misrepresented the data he was presenting. Board members were unaware of the inaccuracy of the information presented, but the superintendent shared with the board that the information was misleading, and he offered to provide a more accurate presentation of the data at the next board meeting. Unfortunately, in the next day's newspaper and on its online service the local media reported the inaccurate data as shared by the community member.

At the following board meeting, the superintendent attempted to correct the misrepresentation of the school's standardized test results, but was constantly interrupted and shouted down by the members of the community who had made up their mind about the data prior to the superintendent's full presentation.

Questions:

1. Who from the school board should respond to public comment? How should the board respond to public comment whether they believe the community member's analysis of the data or not?
2. What steps could the superintendent and school board have taken prior to the board meeting and public comment in order to communicate student information data to the community and possibly avoid this situation?
3. Should the superintendent reach out to the media about its reporting inaccurate data before seeking a comment from the school district or vetting the information that was shared by the community member? Why or why not?
4. How should the school board president have addressed the interruption of the superintendent's presentation?
5. What staff should be present at the public board meeting? Should the entire cabinet be present at the public board meeting?

NOTES

1. National School Boards Association (2020). *The key work of school boards.* Alexandria, VA: NSBA Publication.

2. Holmqvist, M. and Lantz Ekström, M. (2024). A systematic review of research on educational superintendents. *Cogent Education*, 11(1). https://doi.org/10.1080/2331186X.2024.2307142

3. Center for Public Education (2019). *Eight characteristics of effective school boards.* Alexandria, VA: NSBA Publication.

4. Togneri, Wendy and Anderson, Stephen E. (2003). *Beyond islands of excellence: What districts can do to improve instruction and achievement in all schools.* Washington, DC: Learning FIrst Alliance.

Chapter 17

Engaging Administrative Team/Cabinet Members

"If you want to go fast, go alone; if you want to go far, go together."

African Proverb

The superintendent of schools deals with several people, all involved in managing the various components of a job once relegated to one person, the superintendent. However, the days of the one-person operation are nearly over. In most districts, growth has been a factor as districts have become too large and/or multifaceted to maintain a one-person central office. The modern superintendency is far too advanced and has duties too far-reaching for one person to do an adequate job.

For the superintendent and the central office to function effectively and efficiently, many districts have created some type of administrative team or cabinet. Some districts have different teams or cabinets to oversee different areas of need. In many districts it is not unusual for the superintendent to select a superintendent's cabinet. This cabinet may be fairly small in size and generally has a great deal of authority or influence and the "ear" of the superintendent. Because of the important and sometimes confidential nature of the cabinet's agenda, it is imperative to the superintendent that the members be loyal to him or her and share the same vision for the district's future.

The first step in getting the superintendent's cabinet on board and engaged in supporting highly effective governing is to make certain team members are thoroughly grounded in the superintendent's governing philosophy. This requires that the superintendent clearly articulate the fundamental values and principles that he/she holds dear; expect adherence to these values in the governing arena; and take the time to explore with the cabinet the practical application of the superintendent's philosophy in working with the board.

The cabinet also needs a thorough grounding in the operations of the governing process, including what governing means and looks like, the use of committees as a governing tool, and practical ways to provide the board members with satisfying governing experiences.

The cabinet is also a very effective mechanism for actively supporting the board's governing work in a less formal setting, away from the close public scrutiny that occurs at full board meetings. Individual cabinet members can serve as the lead staff to each standing committee, heading a support team. For example, if the committee is taking an in-depth look at an educational program, the cabinet member in charge of curriculum and instruction would serve as the lead staff. Designating a member of the superintendent's cabinet to serve as the lead staff to each committee builds in accountability at the cabinet level, in effect identifying a person whose professional success is publicly tied to the effectiveness of the standing committee rather than the superintendent being the only officer accountable for committee performance.[1]

Finally, board-savvy superintendents always use their cabinets as powerful vehicles for planning, managing, and coordinating the superintendent's board governing programs. This works best when the superintendent serves as the chair and meets at least monthly with his/her cabinet for the purpose of addressing the needs of school board members. According to Eadie,[2] in this capacity, the cabinet is uniquely qualified to play three important roles for the superintendent.

- Assist the superintendent in board capacity building. The regular cabinet meeting focused on governing issues is an ideal setting for discussion of the board-superintendent-cabinet working partnership.
- Provide support for staff heading board committee support teams. The cabinet members leading the committee support team can bring to the full cabinet special issues and concerns that require the support of other administrators or cabinet members.
- Exercise quality control. In light of the stakes involved in supporting the board's governing work, the superintendent will want to have his/her cabinet review and sign off on all documentation being sent to standing committees, making sure that the material is well-crafted, complete, and accurate.

The superintendent's cabinet can be truly effective if they work as a collective team. The governing work is very complex, and it requires the best thinking and effort of everyone in the cabinet. If the members can function as a collective team, the performance of the board-superintendent-cabinet partnership will be healthy and productive.

Scenario:
The superintendent's leadership is not one of authoritarianism and micromanagement, but rather one where building principals are encouraged and supported to engage in transformational leadership. The superintendent has promoted building improvements for staff and students and has stated on several occasions that building principals should be calling on the superintendent's cabinet members for assistance and guidance for such matters as delivering professional development, implementing new instructional strategies, reorganizing accounting practices, administering special education laws and regulations, arranging faculty meetings for success, and so on. Building principals collaborate quite well with cabinet members and have been appreciative of their assistance and guidance, except in one case. The high school principal has been prompted to call upon the superintendent's cabinet for support and guidance, but has been disingenuous in his blaming and criticizing cabinet members when the implementation and follow-up of their support go awry. In his chase to promote himself and get ahead, the high school principal has been holding "clandestine" meetings with the vice president of the school board. Statements have been made by teachers and building administrators to the superintendent and cabinet members about the high school principal's meetings with this board member. Also, confidential information as well as negative comments about cabinet members' support of the high school principal have reached the desks of the superintendent and various cabinet members.

Questions:

1. How should the superintendent be engaged regarding the "clandestine" meetings with the school board members?
2. Should the superintendent address the high school principal and/or the board member? If yes, should the superintendent have anyone else present during the meeting with each individual? What is the role of the board president in this matter?
3. What would be a favorable outcome of each of the meetings?
4. Might the superintendent stand to lose political capital by having a meeting with this board member? Why or why not?

NOTES

1. Sharp, William L. and Walter, James K. (2004). *The school superintendent: The profession and the person.* Lanham, MD: Scarecrow Education.
2. Eadie, Douglas C. (2003). *Eight keys to an extraordinary board-superintendent partnership.* Lanham, MD: Scarecrow Press.

Chapter 18

Managing Crises

"He who fears being conquered is sure to defeat."

Napoleon Bonaparte

Napoleon was a French military officer and statesman who rose to prominence during the French Revolution. He led a series of successful campaigns across Europe during the French Revolutionary and Napoleonic Wars and became the Emperor of the French in the early 19th century.

When it comes to keeping our kids safe, we all have a role to play. For school board members and superintendents, there has never been a time when so much is at stake. Yet, for all the school safety training happening around the country, there is a lack of crisis management training and lessons learned shared with leaders, those with the ultimate responsibility. Many school board members have limited knowledge about the state of school safety, the seriousness of threats impacting schools, and the consequence of changing discipline strategies at odds with the emerging promising practice of threat assessment.

School districts experience a wide variety of crises that have the potential to harm the mental and physical health, learning environment, and safety of students and educators. A school crisis is any traumatic event that seriously disrupts the coping and problem-solving abilities of students and school staff. It is typically sudden, unexpected, dramatic, and forceful and may even threaten survival. A crisis can cause a drastic and tragic change to the environment. It may create a sense of helplessness, hopelessness, and vulnerability combined with a loss of safety.[1] School crises can be on a large scale, such as severe violence, hostage situations, and natural disasters that require an emergency response from the community or they can be more individualized, such as a car accident or the unexpected death of a student or staff member.

Over the last several years, school districts across the country have sought to improve the safety and security of their schools. School districts have partnered with state and local organizations—including law enforcement, emergency management, fire services, hospitals, and local health and mental health departments—to improve the physical infrastructure of school facilities, update emergency plans and procedures, and coordinate a response plan in case of a traumatic event.

According to the U.S. Government Accountability Office,[2] between 2017 and 2022, "over 300 presidentially declared major disasters have occurred across all 50 states and all U.S. territories. Many of these disasters have had devastating effects on K-12 schools, including those in socially vulnerable communities for whom disaster recovery is more challenging." This data underscores the need for superintendents and school boards to adapt their preparedness plans to the evolving landscape of potential emergencies and threats.

In recent decades school administrators at all levels have experienced diverse crises, including, but not limited to, floods, tornados, hurricanes, school shootings, chemical spills, and infectious disease outbreaks. These are just some of the important issues of the day, at a time when school violence is increasing at an alarming rate. School board members and superintendents must be well-versed in school safety because at the end of the day, there is nothing more important than keeping our children safe and it is our school leaders who are held accountable.

The best way to protect students, teachers, and staff while in school buildings and during school-sponsored events is to make sure school districts are prepared. Threats come in many forms, and the community will look to the school board, superintendent, and administrative teams, as the leaders of the district, for reassurance. Having a crisis management plan in place and activating that plan will encourage the community stakeholders to have confidence in the overall safety of the school district. A crisis management plan is a comprehensive document that outlines the procedures and protocols to follow in the event of various types of crises or emergencies within a school or district. School boards, superintendents, and administrative staff members create these plans in coordination and partnership with local law enforcement, emergency responders, district staff, and community members. Once created, a crisis management plan is effective only if the school board, superintendent, and administrative team regularly review and update it based on current information and data.

Rouse[3] suggests that the essential elements of a crisis management plan for school districts include the following:

- Risk Assessment. A risk assessment will identify and evaluate potential risks and hazards that could impact the safety, security, and well-being of students, staff, and visitors within a school district. These assessments should be updated frequently, with results readily available on school websites and social media platforms.
- Crisis Management Team. An Incident Command System (ICS) is a *standardized approach* to managing emergency incidents. It provides a clear chain of command to ensure that all responding agencies and personnel are working together in a coordinated manner to achieve a common goal. Here are the five significant teams within an ICS:

    1. Command—The Command team directs the incident. Here, the Incident Commander sets objectives, determines priorities, and develops a response plan. The Incident Commander also ensures that all resources needed for the response are available and deployed promptly and effectively.
    2. Operations—The Operations staff manages resources, coordinates with personnel, and ensures that response efforts align with the objectives and priorities.
    3. Planning—The Planning team gathers and analyzes information about the incident, determines resource needs, and develops strategies to achieve the objectives set by the Incident Command.
    4. Logistics—The Logistics team acquires and provides resources like equipment, supplies, and facilities for response operations.
    5. Finance/Administration—This team is responsible for managing the financial and administrative aspects of the incident. Team members track expenses and process contracts and agreements to ensure that all documentation related to the incident is maintained.

- Collaboration with Community—School districts cannot manage a crisis alone, and these plans should be created with people who have expertise in crisis response and management: local law enforcement agencies, emergency responders, community mental health organizations, and so on.
- Training—Regular training is an essential element to any successful crisis management plan. All Incident Command Team members should receive training in the National Incident Management System and the ICS. Training and drills can help everyone remember their roles and the procedures needed to follow to stay safe during emergencies. Training sessions should be done calmly to ensure the drills don't traumatize the students.
- Communication Protocols—A proper communication protocol includes who should be informed of the emergency and when. This includes deciding what and when to communicate to parents, community members, and

the media. The more community stakeholders hear from official district sources (school website, social media, etc.), the better.

A crisis management plan should be put in writing, communicated to all staff, and practiced regularly through drills and exercises. School staff should be trained, at least annually, in applicable planning procedures. Today's school boards, superintendents, and administrators are faced not only with external pressures for academic improvement but also with general school safety. Students and staff must feel safe from forces that may compromise their well-being. A sense of security is integral for supporting the school learning environment. Collaboration among and between school board members, superintendents, district administrative teams, school staff, students, parents, and community stakeholders should occur before, rather than during or after, a potential emergency or crisis.[4] Because of the serious nature of an emergency or crisis, the Crisis Management Plan should be one of the first documents reviewed after accepting the role as superintendent.

Scenario:
A suburban school district received a telephone call at 11:10 a.m. with the caller describing an active shooter on the school grounds outside an elementary school. When the superintendent notified local law enforcement about the matter, it was disclosed that there was no immediate report of any shots fired, but local law enforcement reported that an "alleged assailant" was believed to have a firearm and headed toward the schools. The district office said in several posts on Facebook around 11:30 a.m. that students at all of the district's schools were on lockdown and family members were notified to not come to any schools. Law enforcement shared with the superintendent that an initial search of the elementary school did not yield additional suspects, and there was no evidence of any individuals being harmed. Law enforcement further stated that the "alleged assailant" had been neutralized outside the school building. The school district said at 12:30 p.m. in a final post on Facebook that the "alleged assailant" had been taken into custody by local law enforcement and that the lockdown had been lifted. A brief description of the matter was shared on Facebook with parents and the community. However, the police department said it could not immediately provide additional information on the matter and a person who answered the telephone at the district office declined to comment to the media.

Questions:

1. As superintendent of schools, would you have done anything differently during this incident? If yes, please explain.

2. Would this incident serve as a good example for having a crisis management plan in place to refer to during this emergency? Why or why not?
3. Should the superintendent have shared some details of this incident with parents and the community? Why or why not?
4. Should the superintendent have shared any details of this incident with students and staff? Why or why not?
5. What would your next steps be once the incident has ended?

NOTES

1. National Education Association (2018). *NEA's school crisis guide.* Washington, DC: National Education Association.

2. U.S. Government Accountability Office (2022). *Annual report.* Washington, DC: U.S. Government Accountability Office.

3. Rouse, Joseph (2024). *The importance of crisis management and emerging preparedness for superintendents.* Public School WORKS Research and Development Team, Cincinnati, OH: WORKS International.

4. Reeves, Melissa A., Brock, Stephen E., and Cowan, Katherine C. (2008). *Managing school crises: More than just a response.* Washington, DC: Principal Leadership, National Association of Secondary School Principals.

Chapter 19

Keeping Your Bags Packed

"The secret of change is to focus all of your energy not on fighting the old but building the new."

Socrates

Socrates was a great Greek philosopher of the ancient period of Western philosophy. A legendary figure even in his own time, he was admired for his integrity, his self-mastery, his profound philosophical insight, and his great argumentative skill.

The tenure of a superintendent is often less than four years. The tenure coincides with the election of the second set of school board members. The superintendent makes several decisions over the course of a given school year that impact staff, students, and/or teachers. Each decision that is made burns some political capital the superintendent may have banked over time. As a result, the position of superintendent is not for the person who is unwilling or unable to relocate. Superintendents should realize that when they accept this position they work at the whim and will of a small majority. Consequently, the superintendent should know how to count to four when he/she has a seven-member board (or to three for a five-member board). Failure to do this simple math can be detrimental to the superintendent's job and future. Sometimes it does not take long for the majority of the board to turn against a superintendent and vote to dismiss him or her or vote to not renew a contract. While there are many perks to being a superintendent, job security and longevity are not among them. Therefore, figuratively speaking, keep your bags packed.

Superintendents who move into new communities and do not know anyone may be judged by the position they hold. They are strangers with a political base achieved solely through the stature of the position, not from previous relationships. Superintendents can overestimate their influence and forget that typically board members have lived in the same community for years, establishing relationships that allow them to weather political storms that would sink the superintendent. Someone once commented that a new superintendent makes a few friends and a few enemies the first year and the number of enemies grows proportionally to the more challenging decisions the superintendent makes. If this is true, it makes sense the scales will eventually tip against the superintendent causing a rift between the board and the superintendent.

Many superintendents who have been terminated or non-renewed express complete surprise at this outcome. The superintendents often claim that they never saw any warning signs. In reality, there were warning signs that the superintendent either misread, denied, or overlooked. To be terminated is both devastating and demoralizing. It may often be unfair and politically motivated, but sitting superintendents, or aspiring superintendents, must realize the highly visible, highly political job carries a high risk for termination. It is important that the warning signs be noticed, and that the superintendent recognizes the need for coordinated action and damage control.

In 1998, Walter and Carlan[1] grouped these warning signs into four main categories suggesting forthcoming board problems for the superintendent.

Category 1: The superintendent—contract, salary, and evaluation

- The board openly speaks against the superintendent to members of the community and the news media.
- The board makes no move to renew the superintendent's contract.
- The board ceases to give pay raises to the superintendent.
- The board wants to evaluate the superintendent sooner than the contract specifies.
- The board calls unscheduled meetings to discuss the superintendent's evaluation and contract.

Category 2: Superintendent/board/community relationships

- The board members run for election on a platform to oust the superintendent.
- The board moves to prevent the superintendent from building a base of community support.
- The board intentionally makes the superintendent the centerpiece of controversy.
- The board circumvents the superintendent and deals with subordinate administrators.

- The board begins to micromanage the school district.
- The board employs outside consultants to audit the school district operations and evaluate the superintendent's leadership.

Category 3: Superintendent/board meetings

- The board accuses the superintendent of failing to communicate even though board agendas, packets, and supporting information are complete.
- The board tightly controls the board meeting agenda, so the superintendent is placed in a reactive posture necessitating continuous preparation and follow-up of board directives.
- The board designs questions not pertaining to current motions or agenda items to undermine competence and the role of the superintendent.
- The board questions all the superintendent's recommendations.
- The board leaks confidential correspondence to the news media.

Category 4: Superintendent's final days

- The board holds clandestine meetings to discuss dissatisfaction with the superintendent's professional performance.
- The board president does nothing to "gavel down" or prohibit individuals from making personal attacks against the superintendent.
- The board monitors the superintendent's personal and professional life; the board questions every school district expenditure and makes it difficult for the superintendent to leave the school district for personal vacations or professional conferences.
- The superintendent finds administrative team members unavailable to attend regularly scheduled cabinet meetings.
- The superintendent finds work performance affected by the negative atmosphere.

If any of these warning signs occur, it may be time for the superintendent to ask himself/herself a few important questions:

- Is my job in jeopardy?
- Can I do anything to improve my relationship with the board and/or the community?
- Should I seek legal counsel?
- What is the contract language regarding the buy-out or termination?

- What are my time constraints in finding another position?
- What are the risks versus rewards if I stay in this superintendency?

In today's volatile educational climate, it is no longer considered a "failure" to be dismissed by a school board. If the superintendent runs into difficulty with the board, the superintendent may need to cut his/her losses and move on without regret. Being a superintendent offers great personal satisfaction, but the position is both political and perilous. Be alert to the warning signs and know when it is time to search for a new position.

The superintendency continues to be a very functional position in public education. Superintendents across the country are the education leaders of their respective school districts and communities and serve as the main link between the district and the community. Although the data suggest there are ways to improve the relationships between the superintendent and the board of education, most superintendents are in good graces with their boards.

The future of the superintendency seems to be tied more closely than ever to harmonious working relationships with boards and community groups. Successful superintendents will be those who have excellent communication skills, understand instructional processes, and can create functioning coalitions that will ensure the financial and educational survival of the public school system. However, no matter how equipped, savvy, and "perfect fits" superintendents are for a community and its school board, the position remains a political and precarious one that requires superintendents to continue to invest in themselves and to be prepared to get another job before needing to leave the current one, especially if the superintendent's math doesn't add up to a supportive majority of the board.

Scenario:
While serving for the past twelve years as the "perfect fit" district leader, the superintendent was able to tackle the financial deficit, negotiate annual pay increases for all staff, lead the community's passing of two mill levies, provide additional resources to the special needs population, and increase by threefold the donations to the education foundation. However, after the spring break board members of the mid-size school district voted to non-renew the contract of the superintendent.

In the weeks leading up to the non-renewal of the superintendent's contract, the board began to micromanage the operation of the school district and ceased to provide an annual bonus to the superintendent. Despite the superintendent's successes and his desire to remain in his current position, the superintendent agreed to part ways with the school board after hours of negotiations with the school board.

Questions:

1. When board members declare a superintendent candidate as a "perfect fit," what do you think they are referring to?
2. What might a superintendent do to "build" political capital? What might a superintendent do to "burn" political capital? Which is simpler to do, build or burn political capital? Why?
3. Were there "warning signs" the superintendent needed to recognize after twelve years in his role as superintendent? If so, what were the "warning signs?"
4. If you believe there were warning signs, were the warning signs at a low, medium, or high level? Should the superintendent have prepared an exit strategy once he/she completed the work the original board asked the superintendent to address? Why or why not?

NOTE

1. Walter, James K. and Carlan, Catherine (1998). *Telltale warning signs of imminent danger for the school superintendent.* Alexandria, VA: Board & Administrator, July.

Chapter 20

Thinking about Your Legacy

"The great use of life is to spend it for something that will outlast it."

William James

James was an American philosopher and psychologist, and the first educator to offer a psychology course in the United States. He is considered to be a leading thinker of the late nineteenth century, one of the most influential philosophers of the United States, and the "Father of American psychology."

Do you think superintendents in school districts think about their long-term legacies? One survey of urban superintendents in the United States found that the average term of service in a district is 3.6 years. Consequently, superintendents do not have a great deal of time to make a mark on an organization. Even if a superintendent stays in a position for more than four years, few if anyone will be talking about the "old superintendent." The programs that were very thoroughly put into place will have been replaced. The school board that hired the "best superintendent the district has ever had" will be either reelected with a new agenda or defeated by new board members with a different agenda.

That being said, there is always time to build and leave a legacy. Just remember why you chose the field of education and the role of educator as a career. The superintendent's first role was that of a teacher/educator. Once a teacher/educator, always a teacher/educator. Consequently, superintendents like classroom teachers are impact-driven. Educators want to positively affect students' lives and are driven by the goal of using their knowledge and expertise to make a difference for students as education has the power to change lives. The vocation of teaching or being a superintendent is about so much more than a job. It's a calling. It's a mission.

Therefore, knowing your "why" will lead you to leaving a long-term legacy. I had a young man, let's call him Jeff, come to my class in 1986 and my entire outlook on teaching changed forever. Jeff came from a home with a younger sister, no mother, and a father who was abusive. Jeff was his sister's protector and many times his protective instincts required Jeff to stay home from school and tend to his sister. When Jeff did attend school, he was behind in his schoolwork. Consequently, Jeff would act out because of his frustration and feeling that he could not learn. When I would discuss the challenges Jeff posed for me and seek guidance from more experienced administrators, several replied, "You can't save all kids, John."

As Carl W. Buechler stated, "They may forget what you said, they may forget what you did, but they will never forget how you made them feel." There were many days I felt helpless, and I was fighting a losing battle. There were moments of doubt, fear, frustration, and defeat. However, I was committed to walking alongside my students and instilling in them the skills they needed to ensure competence, find their pathway toward proficiency so that they could gain confidence, and achieve success. I felt it was my responsibility to assist Jeff in breaking the cycle of poverty and abuse and demonstrate what a life of "normalcy" looked like. As a superintendent and a teacher, why did I choose a career that is more than just "teaching?" Why did I believe that all kids can learn and be successful? Why did I keep showing up for my students day after day? Why did I commit every new school year to the "Jeffs" in my class, school and/or district? Because Jeff is my "why!"

The authors of *A Leader's Legacy,* Jim Kouzes and Barry Posner, may have said it best when they wrote:

> Each of us lives on in the memories we create, in the systems and practices we set in place (or don't), and in the lives we touch. We guarantee that what people will say about you [when you're gone] will not be about what you achieved for yourself but what you achieved for others. Not how big a campfire you built but how well you kept others warm, how well you illuminated the night to make them feel safe, and how beautiful you left the campsite for those who would come after you to build the next fire.

I realized that the legacy of successful leaders lives on through the people they touch along the way. What is your "why?"

Chapter 21

Analyzing Superintendent Survey Data

"It is a capital mistake to theorize before one has data."

Arthur Conan Doyle

Sir Arthur Conan Doyle was a British writer and physician. He created the character Sherlock Holmes in 1887 for *A Study in Scarlet*, the first of four novels and fifty-six short stories about Holmes and Dr. Watson. The Sherlock Holmes stories are milestones in the field of crime fiction.

The purpose of the survey was to seek information about intentional superintendent preparation and ongoing efforts around the importance of the superintendent-school board relationships. This would include things such as:

- The number of hours in the superintendents' course of study directed toward the importance of the superintendent-school board relationships.
- The comfort or "ready" level of the superintendents when walking into their first superintendency and facing key issues of importance in developing the superintendent-school board relationships.
- The significance of the superintendent-school board relationship in attaining the district's vision and mission.
- The number of hours designated per month/year toward improving the superintendent-school board relationships in their roles.
- The type of activities the superintendents engage in to assist in improving the superintendent-school board relationships.

The author's desired goal was to create a survey that shed light on the need for better preparation of aspiring superintendents for success as well as retool superintendents in the field who were not exposed to methods or strategies in developing a strong, positive working relationship with a group of elected or appointed citizens who serve as the superintendent's supervisor. Citizens who may not be familiar with creating policies or working collectively to make decisions.

The superintendent survey was shared with two former colleagues who agreed to distribute the survey to currently practicing superintendents in Illinois and Colorado. Also, superintendents were selected from Arkansas, Georgia, Indiana, and North Carolina. All superintendents were randomly selected by accessing email addresses that were available on the statewide Department of Education sites. The survey was presented as an online survey with three weeks to complete the thirteen-question survey with respondents remaining anonymous.

Overall, the survey was randomly distributed to 858 superintendents with 118 superintendents returning the survey. The overall response rate was 13.8 percent. Seventy-one percent of the respondents have served in the role of superintendent for nine years or less; 78.3 percent have a student enrollment of 4,000 students or less; and 77.9 percent consider their school district to be in a rural setting. The level of education for the respondents consists of 58.5 percent of the superintendents having earned an Ed.D./Ph.D., 28.8 percent an Ed.S., and the remaining earned an M.S. or M.A.

When superintendents were asked how many hours in their course of study were designated toward explaining or preparing them for the importance of superintendent-school board relationships, 56.8 percent of the superintendents stated that four hours or less were designated toward explaining or preparing them for the importance of superintendent-school board relationships, however, 97.5 percent of the superintendents rated the superintendent-school board relationships as being most important or very important in attaining the school district's vision and mission. Furthermore, 78.8 percent of superintendents responded that since becoming a superintendent they spend a minimum of two hours per month (minimum of twenty-four hours per year) engaging in activities to assist in improving the superintendent-school board relationships. The respondents listed such activities as attending school board conferences with board members, establishing work sessions to engage in growth opportunities with the board, holding individual or small group meetings with board members (as the law allows), and hiring consultants to help enhance superintendent-school board relationships. Finally, when superintendents rank ordered actions requiring their attention from most comfortable to least comfortable when they walked into their first superintendency, 75.4 percent of superintendents responded that the least comfortable action requiring the superintendents' attention was dealing with board members who wish to micromanage the daily operations of the school district followed by; establishing clear roles and responsibilities with board members; and tackling the nuances of the politics of the job.

The responses provided by the superintendents about working with and addressing the needs of the board of education highlight the importance of the superintendent-school board relationship. When superintendents were asked to rank order from 1 to 5, with 1 being the least persuasive reason to seek a new position and 5 being the most persuasive reason to seek a new position, superintendents overwhelmingly responded with 77.8 percent of their responses stating that the most persuasive reason to seek a new position was the school board becoming unreasonable in its expectations.

Superintendents were asked on a scale from 1 to 5, with 1 being not prepared and 5 being very well prepared, how well prepared they were for their first superintendent position. Sixty-seven percent of superintendents responded that they were not prepared, slightly prepared, or somewhat prepared.

With the graying of the profession and the need for exemplary school superintendents, the preparation of school superintendents who can successfully lead school districts is vitally important. Fry, Bottoms, O'Neill, and Walker[1] contend that too many administrative preparation programs offer last century curriculum, do not spend enough time helping aspiring school leaders develop competencies, and fail to assure the intern is given a rich and meaningful experience. In a study by Levine,[2] a majority of school leaders who were surveyed indicated that their programs did not prepare graduates to cope with administrative realities, including superintendent-school board relationships. A study by Davis[3] (2016) showed that a majority of superintendents surveyed on university preparation programs indicated that program improvements were necessary. The research said that district leaders rated the level of preparation as "less than effective" on the competencies needed by school leaders. The study further defined the content areas that were lacking in existing preparation programs as being labor relations, interpersonal skills and group dynamics, special education, crisis management, school finance, community relations, and relationships with the board of education members. In addition, several members of the study recommended that the requirements for clinical and field experiences be increased.

Superintendents were asked to reflect on their past or present superintendent's position and offer the advice or training they wished they would have had before beginning their first superintendency. Overwhelmingly, the following three responses surfaced as the most valuable recommendations:

- setting clear expectations with the board/discussing the role of the board,
- addressing the micromanaging of board members, and
- seeking a strong mentor or cohort group to assist with collaboration, provide guidance, and allow a safe environment for venting frustration.

Given the fact that the superintendent serves at the discretion of the board of education and the average tenure for a school superintendent is less than four years, the author felt it was important to ask currently practicing superintendents about the old adage, "keep your bags packed." Sometimes it does not take long for the majority of the board to turn against a superintendent and vote to dismiss him or her or vote to not renew his/her contract. While there are many perks to being a superintendent, job security and longevity are not among them. Therefore, figuratively speaking, do superintendents "keep their bags packed?" The question was asked of participating superintendents on a scale of 1 to 5, with 1 being never and 5 being always, how often do you feel a need to "keep your bags packed?" Sixty-two percent of the superintendents responded that they rarely or never consider the need to "keep their bags packed." However, almost 40 percent of respondents felt a need to sometimes, often, or always "keep their bags packed." Superintendents realize that when they accept this position they work at the pleasure of the board. They also know that many of their decisions rarely have the support of the majority of the community's stakeholders. Consequently, it is said that superintendents "burn" more political capital than they build over time, which tips the scales against the superintendent causing friction between the board and the superintendent.

As today's educational landscape gets more complex, the data support the need for superintendent preparation programs to focus on content that will encourage and develop methodology that addresses the importance of the superintendent-school board relationships. Also, the data support the need to assist superintendents in creating effective strategies for working with school board members and to guide superintendents throughout the day-to-day operations while avoiding potential occasions for disaster. Finally, the data support the need for superintendents and school board members to increase the type of activities that the parties engage in order to improve the superintendent-school board relationships.

NOTES

1. Fry, Betty, Bottoms, Gene, O'Neill, Kathy, and Walker, Susan (2007). *Schools need good leaders now: State progress in creating a learning-centered school leadership system.* Atlanta, GA: Southern Regional England Board.
2. Levine, Arthur (2005). *Educating school leaders.* Washington, DC: The Education Schools Project.
3. Davis, Jacquelyn (2016). *Improving university superintendent/principal preparation programs: Five themes from the field.* New York, NY: The Wallace Foundation.

Appendix A
Thought-Provoking Scenarios

1. *Scenario:*
   A board candidate made a public statement during his campaign for an open school board seat that he thought the "school district had too many administrators and the administrators salaries were too high." The candidate was able to get the media to print his statement without the media vetting his comment. The data showed that the district had an equivalent number of administrators as compared to the other school districts in the region and districts with similar student populations throughout the state and the administrators' salaries were equally in line with other appropriate comparisons. However, the data did not stop the candidate from continuing to make his claims of the district having too many administrators and that the administrators were being paid too much money. Upon being seated as a newly elected school board member, he requested from the superintendent a listing of the number of administrators, their respective positions/titles, and their salaries. The new board member did not request any comparison data.

   Questions:

   a. What role, if any, does the superintendent have in providing the actual data to this board member? To whom should the superintendent provide the data?
   b. Does the board president have a role to play in this matter? If yes, what is the board president's role?
   c. Does the full board have a role to play in this matter? If yes, what is the role of the full board?

d. Should the superintendent address the leadership team regarding the newly elected board's comments? If yes, what steps should the superintendent take with the leadership team?
2. *Scenario:*
   A veteran board member has a child who qualifies for special education services. As a parent, the board member has approved an Individual Education Plan for her child. The veteran board member also serves as an advocate for other parents in the school district who have children who qualify for special education services. The board member regularly approaches the director of special education requesting individual aides for numerous students receiving special education services, although it has been determined by a special education team that the students in question do not qualify for such services. When the director of special education and his team do not approve the veteran board member's requests for individual aides for students, the board member repeatedly tells the superintendent that the director of special education needs to be terminated.

   Questions:

   a. What, if any, are the conflicts of interests in this scenario?
   b. How should the superintendent address the veteran board member? Who, if anyone, should be present during a conversation between the veteran board member and the superintendent?
   c. Is it appropriate for a board member to approach the superintendent and request that an employee be terminated? Why or why not?
   d. What are some steps that could be taken to improve the relationship between the board member serving as a special education advocate and the administrative team?
3. *Scenario:*
   A relatively new superintendent wrote an annual performance evaluation of one of the principals. The evaluation was not completely glowing as the superintendent thought there were some areas for growth. While the principal was not a candidate for demotion or termination, the superintendent felt that some aspects of the principal's work could be better. The evaluation conference included a discussion of the principal's strengths, areas for growth, and steps that could be taken to address the concerns. The principal thanked the superintendent for the feedback, something that had apparently been lacking with the previous superintendent.

   The principal was popular with his students, staff, and parents. He had also become somewhat close with one of the board members. To the superintendent's surprise, the principal went to a board member shortly after the evaluation conference. The board member met with the principal and told him not to worry as the board member felt the principal was doing a good job. It appeared that the principal wanted to build a coalition with some of the board in case he needed support should there not be improvement that satisfied the superintendent.*

Questions:

a. By taking his concerns about the superintendent's evaluation of his performance to a board member, did the principal handle this situation appropriately? Why or why not? Based on what you know of the board member's reaction, did the board member handle this situation appropriately? Why or why not?
b. As a result of the principal taking his concerns about his evaluation to a board member, how should the superintendent address this matter with the principal?
c. With whom on the school board should the superintendent address this situation—the one board member, the full board, the one board member and the board president, or the board president? Why?
d. What action steps can be taken by the superintendent to avoid similar situations from occurring in the future?

4. *Scenario:*

A rapidly growing school district faced challenging issues. The new superintendent found that little long-range planning had been done including long-term facility plans and lack of acquiring available resources from the state. One board member talked about significant challenges as schools would become overcrowded and there would be a shortage of teachers. These observations were shared with the entire board and the superintendent was directed to investigate the potential future growth and report back to the board in one month. Being the take-charge person she was, the superintendent sprang into action. After all her research, the superintendent concluded that the district would need land for building more schools. She consulted the county supervisor prior to drafting a plan. The superintendent determined that there were several ideal school sites, but she did not know if there were political complications with any of these sites. The superintendent believed that the county supervisor would be the best person to advise her, and he proved to be very familiar and knowledgeable about the district and county. The superintendent called the board president to set up a meeting as she was excited to debrief the board president about the meeting she had with the county supervisor and to share the details of the plan she had developed. After eagerly sharing her plan with the board president, the board president said, "How could you have done something so blatantly foolish? Do you not know that the county supervisor is running for reelection and will probably be opposed by one of the board members? He was helpful because he wants to win reelection at the expense of one of our board members. Now the problem is getting the board members to support the use of the county supervisor and the plan you created."*

Questions:

a. Who is the superintendent's first source for defining and debriefing challenging issues facing the school district? Why?
b. Superintendents are take-charge people and eager to make things happen in a positive, expeditious manner. In this case, how should the superintendent have proceeded?
c. Were there political implications related to this incident? If so, what were the political implications? How could they impact the board? How could they impact the superintendent?
d. Even when pressed with an urgent problem, with whom should the superintendent cross-check his/her knowledge and information to avoid surprises? Why?

5. *Scenario:*

A board member returned from a state board member conference with the idea and example of how to evaluate the board's own performance. The other board members reluctantly agreed to try to use the generic evaluation form. The process required board members to respond to statements using a rating scale and provide comments if they cared to do so. The board directed the superintendent to compile the data and send the report back to all the board members. A real difficulty emerged with the process. It put the superintendent in a delicate situation because one board member used the process to attack other board members straining board member relationships. The superintendent made an executive decision and decided not to send the full report to all board members.*

Questions:

a. Should the only evaluation of board members be determined by the voters every four years? Why or why not?
b. Does the superintendent have a role to play in the board's evaluation of its own performance? Why or why not?
c. What problems arose for the board from the idea and example of how to evaluate the board's own performance?
d. Although the self-evaluation process offered by the board member returning from a state board member conference did not work, should

the superintendent propose other examples of board self-evaluation processes? Why or why not?

6. *Scenario:*

A school board sought the services of a superintendent search firm to recruit, develop, and retain a new leader to "improve the district's student outcomes." The search firm stated in its brochure that through its collaborative, research-based approach in the search process, it matches the "right leader with the goals and priorities of the school system and community." One of the school board's most pressing priorities was to address the declining student enrollment and the budget deficit. The board retained a new superintendent and gave him the charge of tackling this priority. The board's solution to reducing its operating costs and saving future dollars was to close and consolidate schools, which proved to be very divisive for the parents and the community. After two years of challenging work, the superintendent and the board successfully closed and consolidated schools and saved the school district several million dollars in the operation of its budget. The next election in November saw the election of three new board members who disagreed with the consolidation of schools. At the first meeting of the new board members in January, the board's first action of business was to fire the superintendent.

Questions:

a. What could the superintendent or board have done to ensure a more favorable response from the parents and community regarding the consolidation of schools?
b. What types of challenges are created when new board members form a majority and at its first board meeting in the middle of the school year vote to terminate the superintendent?
c. In terms of the superintendent-board relationship, where did the partnership break down leading to the dismissal of the superintendent?
d. Barring the superintendent being involved in something unethical or unlawful, what are the negative impacts to a school district or community when a superintendent is dismissed or fired?
e. Who benefits when leadership is changed?

* Excerpts of scenarios were gathered from Townsend, Rene S., Johnston, Gloria L., Gross, Gwen E., Lynch, Peggy, Garcy, Lorraine M., Roberts, Benita B., and Novotney, Patricia B. (2007). *Effective superintendent-school board practices: strategies for developing and maintaining good relationships with your board.* Thousand Oaks, CA: Corwin Press.

Appendix B
Author's Thoughts on the Scenarios

The author selected a question from each scenario to offer his perspective. Because each school district and community are unique (i.e., protocols, policies, superintendent or board experience, superintendent or board longevity, community involvement), responses to questions may vary.

Chapter 2 Scenario
Question 1:
What could the board have done differently throughout the process to ensure a successful outcome?
Author's Thought:
The board president (or a third party) could have facilitated more discussion among board members to eliminate differences, find commonalities, or seek compromises around a favored finalist. If, after more dialogue among board members, a more unanimous finalist could not be identified, the board should have requested the professional search firm to restart the superintendent search.

Chapter 3 Scenario
Question 3:
What steps might the superintendent have followed in an effort to avoid a confrontation with the board leading up to the contract non-renewal of the veteran administrator?
Author's Thought:
The superintendent could have coordinated regular scheduled check-in meetings with the board president to review his/her areas of improvement—"failing to address previously documented insufficient leadership practices including multiple years of well below average student achievement." During the regular scheduled check-in meetings, the superintendent could have

demonstrated that he/she took the notice to improve seriously by providing the board president with evidence of steps he/she has taken to address the areas of improvement. Hopefully by the end of year, the superintendent would have addressed all of his/her areas of improvement and have supporting documentation of his/her improvements. The superintendent's documents could then be distributed to all board members for their review prior to the superintendent's annual evaluation assessment.

Chapter 4 Scenario
Question 1:
Confidential information being shared in the public domain reaches the superintendent's desk. How should the superintendent handle this new knowledge?
Author's Thought:
The superintendent needed to clarify what confidential information was shared and who was responsible for sharing this information. Once it was discovered that the confidential information was shared by two board members, the superintendent needed to contact the board president. The superintendent may assist the board president, as appropriate, in gathering the facts; however, it should be the board president's role to discuss with the two board members their failure to follow board protocol and policy in regard to confidential information.

Chapter 5 Scenario
Question 4:
If role confusion exists in your district, can you describe where the breakdown is occurring?
Author's Thought:
It is not uncommon to observe the superintendent and the board exchanging roles. Superintendents have been known to create board policy and board members have been known to get engaged in the daily operations of the school district. The superintendent needs to hold the board accountable to stay in its leadership lane and the board president needs to hold the superintendent accountable for similar behavior. Usually, the superintendent and board president work together to see that role confusion is significantly reduced or eliminated.

Chapter 6 Scenario
Question 4:
What could the superintendent or board president have done to ensure the board's readiness to vote in favor of the following year's budget?
Author's Thought:
It appears that the superintendent and the board president were on the same page when it came to placing the following year's budget on the board's

agenda. However, the superintendent and the board president did not permit enough time for individual board members to express their concerns or provide input for their priorities to be considered for inclusion in the following year's budget. The superintendent or board president should have intentionally asked individual board members where each stood on his/her comfort level with the budget moving forward.

Chapter 7 Scenario
Question 1:
What should be the board president's response to the parents? What should be the board president's response to the board member who made the motion?
Author's Thought:
The board president should thank the parents for sharing their concerns regarding the lack of students of color enrolled in AP classes. It is a protocol for board members to not respond to speakers during public comment. The board president should remind the board member who made the motion to "eliminate AP classes" that there is a proper procedure to follow when making a motion on a topic of interest; share the process the board member failed to follow; and ask the full board if there is an interest in requesting the superintendent to investigate the demographics for all K–12 enriched/advanced classes and how the schools determine student placements into these programs.

Chapter 8 Scenario
Question 2:
What, if anything, could the school board do moving forward to address community concerns?
Author's Thought:
The school board could form a community advisory committee that would work with the school board to address community concerns and provide feedback on important decisions. The committee would be made up of parents, students, teachers, and community leaders. The community advisory committee can play a key role in providing feedback and suggestions to the school board, which can help the board make better decisions that are aligned with the needs of the community. This action can assist the board in rebuilding trust and transparency with the community.

Chapter 9 Scenario
Question 2:
Is there a good working relationship between the superintendent and the board? What accounts for the relationship being good or poor?
Author's Thought:

A positive working relationship between the superintendent and the board is built when opportunities arise for both parties to spend time together getting to know one another in a social and professional setting. The superintendent's job is very diverse and complex, and the board's responsibilities are immense. Committing to collaborate during work sessions, board retreats, executive sessions, school board conferences, district social events, and so on allows both parties to gain a richer understanding of how best to support and partner with one another.

Chapter 10 Scenario
Question 2:
From the superintendent's perspective, what are the challenges with having board members serve on a bargaining team? What are the benefits of having board members serve on a bargaining team?
Author's Thought:
The challenge for the superintendent when board members serve on the negotiating team is to keep the conversations on track. The teachers can view the board members' presence as an opportunity to air all of their grievances and complaints, many of which do not belong at the negotiating table. Also, the board members' presence can be somewhat distracting as teachers will want to address their concerns directly to the board members forgetting other negotiating team members are present. The benefit for the superintendent when board members serve on the negotiating team can be that trust is enhanced between the two parties. When board members hear directly from the teachers or participate in the conversations, the teachers feel more valued and trust increases. Also, board members' presence allows members to gather a firsthand account of how the teachers feel about issues as some issues are more important to the teachers than others. Finally, when board members serve on the negotiating team it may strengthen the trust between the superintendent and board members as non-attending board members can hear from their colleagues about the process and the issues being raised thus helping reduce rumors, innuendos, and accusations.

Chapter 11 Scenario
Question 1:
Should the superintendent seek an opportunity to express his/her views and recommendations before the vote of the school board on this matter? If not, why not? If yes, what should the superintendent recommend?
Author's Thought:
With the board conducting negotiations with the teacher union in this district and the superintendent being an inactive participant, the superintendent may be able to serve as a neutral third party and manage a compromise between the two parties. The superintendent could convince the board to forgo its

scheduled closed-door session where it was to consider taking action against the teachers and encourage the teachers' union to instruct its members to attend the "back-to-school night." This agreement would allow both parties to maintain the appearance of working together while preserving the trust between the parents and the teachers.

Chapter 12 Scenario
Question 1:
Were the school district and the individual schools utilizing the local media to their benefit? If not, what could the district do to expand media coverage, especially in increasing stories that highlight effective programs?
Author's Thought:
The superintendent could communicate with the local media on the types of stories they would cover about the schools; the length of a written article they would accept; and the style of pictures to include with the written stories. A schedule could be created for the district asking each school on a rotating basis to submit an article highlighting programs and students to the media. Also, schools could call or send a calendar of monthly events the local media could attend for possible newsworthy stories. Whatever the district can do to make the job simpler and smoother for the local media will help to build a stronger relationship with the local media.

Chapter 13 Scenario
Question 5:
What would have created a successful process for the unveiling of the purpose of the District Accountability Committee and the board's expectations for the standing committee going forward?
Author's Thought:
The board of education should have made a "big splash" with the creation of the District Accountability Committee. The board should have taken every opportunity to promote the new committee (board meetings, district and school newsletters, web page and social media, local media, PTOs, etc.) and highlight the requirements for becoming a member of the committee. In the explanation of the expectations, the board should have established a deadline for receiving the names of interested parents and community members who would like to serve, announce when the committee would be approved by the board, and share in its explanation the date of the first meeting of the committee. If the board had taken control of the narrative of the forming of the committee, it would have saved itself the embarrassment of well-meaning parents launching their own committee without board input or approval.

Chapter 14 Scenario
Question 2:
What can you derive from the actions of the teachers' association regarding the process for the "vote of no confidence" and the communication procedures that were followed?
Author's Thought:
My takeaways from the action of the high school teachers' association members are that:

- they did not want the superintendent to know what they had planned so that he/she could not intervene and work with the local teachers' association board and the regional union representative to find a compromise to the high school teachers' grievance(s).
- they wanted to create a story with an element of surprise and by immediately sharing their actions with the media, the teachers were hopeful that it would provide them with some leverage moving forward with their grievance(s).
- at least some of the teachers were probably hopeful their action would be enough to lead the high school principal to resign or be dismissed.

Chapter 15 Scenario
Question 1:
What steps can the superintendent take in order to bring the new board member into the school system? What steps can the superintendent take to make the new board member a positive contributor?
Author's Thought:
The board of education with assistance from the superintendent should have a well-designed onboarding process for new board members. It would be helpful if all new board members began their roles having an understanding of school board policies, board/district protocols, and pertinent state laws that apply to school board members. The superintendent should meet regularly with the new board members and engage in conversations about her agenda, what the superintendent can do to assist with her agenda, and how her agenda fits into the district mission, values, and goals. By creating opportunities for dialogue, the superintendent can develop a positive working relationship and trust with the new board member. The stronger the relationship between the superintendent and the new board member, the more likely she will listen to and work with the superintendent and collaborate with her colleagues.

Chapter 16 Scenario
Question 2:
What steps could the superintendent and school board have taken prior to the board meeting and public comment in order to communicate student information data to the community and possibly avoid this situation?
Author's Thought:
The superintendent could have arranged with the board president that any new testing or school data that is received from the state department of education automatically be placed on the next board agenda. It is best that new data received in the district office be shared by the administrative team in its complete form. The board and superintendent would want to have the initial control over the testing or school data narrative to be certain the information is shared with accuracy and transparency. The community or parents can ask questions about the presented data or report or even provide their own interpretation, but the district should always be out front on certain topics and testing or school data would be one such topic.

Chapter 17 Scenario
Question 1:
How should the superintendent be engaged regarding the "clandestine" meetings with the school board members?
Author's Thought:
The superintendent should meet with the board president and share with him/her the facts as the superintendent knows them regarding the clandestine meetings. It should be the responsibility of the board president to have a conversation with his/her board colleague regarding the secret meetings with the high school principal. The superintendent also should meet with the high school principal. As the high school principal's supervisor, the superintendent should reinforce the chain of command if the principal has an issue or concern regarding personnel or other matters of importance in his/her building. The high school principal should be reminded that it is the superintendent's role and responsibility to discuss matters of concern with the board and not the high school principal. The high school principal should be notified that his/her failure to follow protocol, chain of command, and/or the superintendent's directive may lead to disciplinary action up to and including dismissal.

Chapter 18 Scenario
Question 5:
What would your next steps be once the incident is brought to an end?
Author's Thought:
After the team has brought the incident to its end, an Incident Commander reviews the results. They go through post-mortem reports thoroughly to

evaluate the team's performance and determine if the objectives of the incident were met. Incident Commanders also arrange a post-mortem meeting where they discuss everything about the incident, from why it occurred, what was done to resolve it, and what the team can learn from it. This helps them prepare for handling similar incidents in the future.

Chapter 19 Scenario
Question 1:
When board members declare a superintendent candidate as a "perfect fit," what do you think they are referring to?
Author's Thought:
When determining whether a person is the right "fit" for a position, the board members are not only assessing the superintendent's skill level and on-the-job competencies, but they are also on the lookout for the right "fit" for that particular role. Being a good fit for a job means having the ability and experience to carry out the job duties, but it also means having the right combination of soft skills, character traits, and career goals that align with the mission and values of the organization and fits in well within the existing school district culture.

Appendix A Scenario 1
Question (b):
Does the board president have a role to play in this matter? If yes, what is the board president's role?
Author's Thought:
The board president should meet with the new board member and share with him/her the protocol that has been established for requesting information. Usually, all board members' requests flow through the board president, so the president is aware of the request; can be certain the request is appropriate; can make certain the superintendent and his/her administrative team are not overwhelmed with untimely or unnecessary requests; and can make certain that all board members receive the same information.

Appendix A Scenario 2
Question (b):
How should the superintendent address the veteran board member? Who, if anyone, should be present during a conversation between the veteran board member and the superintendent?
Author's Thought:
Actually, the board president should be the one to address the veteran board member. The veteran board member serving as an advocate for families who have children with special needs is terrific, but serving as an advocate in the school district where she is serving as a school board member is a conflict of interest. The board president can applaud her efforts as an advocate, but

communicate to her that her advocacy work in the school district where she is serving as a school board member should cease.

Appendix A Scenario 3
Question (a):
By taking his concerns about the superintendent's evaluation of his performance to a board member, did the principal handle this situation appropriately? Why or why not? Based on what you know of the board member's reaction, did the board member handle this situation appropriately? Why or why not?

Author's Thought:
The principal's supervisor and evaluator was the superintendent. The superintendent provided the principal with feedback which included areas of strengths and areas of growth as well as strategies for improving his performance. The principal had several opportunities to ask the superintendent for clarification or continue to have dialogue about his concerns. Unfortunately, the principal chose to bypass discussing concerns about his evaluation with the supervisor and ignored the chain of command. The principal should not have contacted the board member or attempted to schedule a meeting to discuss his evaluation. When the principal contacted the board member and asked the board member to meet with him to discuss his evaluation, the board member should have directed the principal back to the superintendent who serves as his supervisor/evaluator.

Appendix A Scenario 4
Question (b):
Superintendents are take-charge people and eager to make things happen in a positive, expeditious manner. In this case, how should the superintendent have proceeded?

Author's Thought:
The new superintendent was asked to investigate possible school sites for future school facilities and get back to the board. The purchase of several acres of land in a community for a public facility such as a school is an issue that requires confidentiality in order to maintain a fair market for the land, reduce competition, and allow the school board to develop a plan of action before going to the public. Being a new superintendent, she did not know who the key "movers and shakers" in the community were and stated that she was unaware if there would be political complications with the school sites she had selected. The superintendent should have created check-in meetings with the board president to provide updates and ask clarifying questions of the plan prior to the full board update in a month. The superintendent was too eager to have the entire plan completed before engaging the board in a conversation about her progress and discussing the next steps.

Appendix A Scenario 5
Question (a):
Should the only evaluation of board members be determined by the voters every four years? Why or why not?
Author's Thought:
All levels of public education should have high expectations of shared accountability and engage in continuous improvement models on an annual basis, including the board of education. Board self-evaluation tools are helpful in identifying the board's strengths while finding areas of improvement. The self-evaluation will provide governing boards with the tools to identify challenges early on and develop strategies to address those challenges in the interest of maximizing efficiency; unearth new issues to a board or may reveal the "elephant in the room" that everyone knows about, but ignores; refresh the board's understanding of its role and responsibilities; build trust, respect, and communication among board members, the board president, and the superintendent; and allow individual board members to assess their own contributions and work more effectively as a part of a team.

Appendix A Scenario 6
Question (b):
What types of challenges are created when new board members form a majority and at its first board meeting in the middle of the school year vote to terminate the superintendent?
Author's Thought:
Each change in leadership creates a replacement or redirection of core practices and reforms disrupting the stability of leadership for staff, students, and the entire school community. The superintendent being dismissed at the first board meeting of new board members who have a majority creates mistrust and division among and between board members. New board members who are quick to form a coalition tend to be single-issue board members who seek greater control in the decision-making of the daily operations of the district. They fail to see the "big picture" of leading a school district and the complexities that accompany this leadership responsibility. They take on a micromanagement style that is not inclusive of others' ideas and suggestions which can generate a very stressful working environment. If employees are placed in a perpetual defensive posture making it difficult to collaborate, don't be surprised if the teachers' association becomes upset and frustrated by the new majority's leadership and casts a vote of "no confidence" in the board.

Appendix C
Questions for Practicing Superintendents and Data Summary Table

The purpose of this survey is to gather responses from currently practicing superintendents regarding the level of preparation (formal training or coursework) he/she had prior to signing his/her first contract as the district leader. Also, when collecting data regarding formal training or coursework, questions will be asked of current superintendents if developing a relationship with board members is viewed as important and if so, how superintendents go about building these important relationships in their current role.

The data collected will be disaggregated and the findings reported in a published book; however, the respondent will remain anonymous, and all data associated with each respondent will remain confidential.

1. How many years have you served as a superintendent?
   _____ 1–4 years
   _____ 5–9 years
   _____ 10–14 years
   _____ 15–19 years
   _____ 20+ years
2. What is the current student enrollment of the school district where you are serving?
   _____ 1–999
   _____ 1000–3999
   _____ 4000–6999
   _____ 7000–9999
   _____ 10,000+

3. Which best describes your school district?
   _____ Urban
   _____ Suburban
   _____ Rural
4. What is your highest level of education?
   _____ B.S./B.A.
   _____ M.S./M.A.
   _____ Ed.S.
   _____ Ed.D./Ph.D.
5. How many hours in your course of study were designated toward explaining or preparing you for the importance of superintendent-school board relationships?
   _____ 0 hours
   _____ 1–2 hours
   _____ 3–4 hours
   _____ 5–6 hours
   _____ 7–8 hours
   _____ 9–10 hours
   _____ 11+ hours
6. Since becoming superintendent, how important are the superintendent-school board relationships in attaining the district's vision and mission? (On a scale from 1 to 5, with 5 most important, 4 very important, 3 somewhat important, 2 slightly important, and 1 being least important.)

   _____

7. Since becoming superintendent, how many hours per year do you designate toward improving the superintendent-school board relationships?
   _____ 0 hours
   _____ 1–2 hours
   _____ 3–4 hours
   _____ 5–6 hours
   _____ 7–8 hours
   _____ 9–10 hours
   _____ 11+ hours
8. What type of activities do you engage in to assist in improving the superintendent-school board relationships? (Please check all that apply)
   _____ Attend school board conferences with board members.
   _____ Hire consultants to help enhance superintendent-school board relationships.
   _____ Establish work sessions to engage in growth opportunities with the board.
   _____ Hold individual or small group meetings with board members (as the law allows).

_____ The superintendent and board do not engage in such activities.
Please list other activities not listed _____
_____
_____

9. Rank order the items below from most comfortable (10) to least comfortable (1) when walking into your first superintendent position.
   _____ Attending to the Budget and Finances
   _____ Answering Questions Posed by the Media
   _____ Dealing with Board Members Who Wish to Micromanage the Daily Operations
   _____ Communicating with All Stakeholders
   _____ Addressing the Expectations and Mandates of State and Federal Governments
   _____ Working with an Elected (or appointed) Board
   _____ Tackling the Nuances of the Politics of the Job
   _____ Orienting Newly Elected Board Members
   _____ Establishing Clear Roles and Responsibilities with Board Members
   _____ Dealing with Angry Parents and Community Members

10. On a scale from 1 to 5, with 5 being very well prepared, 4 moderately prepared, 3 somewhat prepared, 2 slightly prepared, and 1 not well prepared, how prepared overall were you for your first superintendent position?
    _____

11. If or when you think about seeking a new superintendent position, please rank order from 1 to 5, with 5 being the most persuasive reason to seek a new position, 4 very persuasive, 3 somewhat persuasive, 2 slightly persuasive, and 1 the least persuasive reason to seek a new position.
    _____ I've accomplished all that I can at this time.
    _____ The parents and community have become difficult to work with.
    _____ The board has become unreasonable in its expectations.
    _____ The local media is relentless in its negative reporting about the schools.
    _____ The staff and/or teachers' union have become less interested in collaborating.
    _____ Other (please list) _____
    _____

12. Reflecting on your past or present superintendent's position, what advice or training do you wish you would have had before beginning your first superintendency?

_____
_____
_____

13. The superintendent serves at the discretion of the board of education, and the average tenure of the superintendent is less than four years. There is an old adage, "Keep your bags packed" as you work at the will of a small majority. On a scale from 1 to 5, with 5 being always, 4 often, 3 sometimes, 2 rarely, and 1 never, how often do you feel a need to "keep your bags packed?"

_____

SUPERINTENDENT SURVEY DATA SUMMARY TABLE

Survey Question	Survey Response
Survey randomly distributed to 858 superintendents Survey returned by 118 superintendents	13.8% rate of survey return
Number of years serving as superintendent	71.3% have been in the role for 9 years or less
Current student enrollment in the school district where the superintendent is serving	78.3% have a student enrollment of 4,000 students or less
Best describes the type of school district	77.9% describe school district as rural
Highest level of superintendent education	58.8% Ed.D./Ph.D. 41.2% M.A./M.S.
Number of hours in the course of student designated toward preparing for the importance of superintendent-school board relationship	56.8% stated 4 hours or less in preparation
Rank order the importance of the superintendent-school board relationship in attaining the school district's vision and mission	97.5% ranked the relationship as very important or important
Number of hours as superintendent engaged in activities to improve the superintendent-school board relationship	78.8% stated minimum of 2 hours per month or 24 hours per year

(Continued)

Survey Question	Survey Response
Rank order the most comfortable to least comfortable actions requiring the superintendent's attention	75.4% ranked the least comfortable action was dealing with board members who wish to micromanage the daily operations
Rank order very well prepared to not prepared when stepping into first superintendent position	67.2% ranked being not prepared, slightly prepared, or somewhat prepared for their first superintendent position
Rank order the most persuasive to least persuasive reason to leave the superintendent position	77.8% ranked the most persuasive reason to leave the superintendent position was the school board becoming unreasonable with expectations

Bibliography

Alsbury, Thomas L. (2008). Hitting a moving target: How politics determines the changing roles of superintendents and school boards. In *Handbook of education politics, and policy*. 2nd Edition. New York: Routledge, pp. 37–61.

Alsbury, Thomas L. and Gore, P. (2015). *Improving school boards effectiveness: A balanced governance approach*. Cambridge, MA: Harvard Education Press.

Ashley, Lloyd W. (1968). *The effective school board member*. Danville, IL: Interstate Publishers.

Association of California School Administrator (2023). *10 tips for superintendents signing their first contract*. Sacramento, CA: ACSA.

Association of Wisconsin School Administration (2009). *Ten of the most common superintendent interviewing mistakes*. Madison, WI: AWSA.

Balch, B. V. (2018). *Building great school board-superintendent teams: A systemic approach to balancing roles and responsibilities*. Bloomington, IN: Solution Tree.

Blackburn, Barbara R. and Williamson, Ronald (2019). *5 Keys to handling the media for school leaders*. Washington, DC: edCircuit.

Blumberg, Arthur and Blumberg, Phyllis (1985). *The school superintendent: Living with conflict*. New York: Teachers College Press.

Board of Education (2021). *Request for proposal from superintendent search firm*. Champaign, IL: Champaign Unit 4 School District.

BoardSource (2022). *Do we really need board committees?* Washington, DC: Leading with Intent.

Boyd, William Lowe and Miretzky, Debra (2003). *American education governance on trial: Change and challenges*. Chicago, IL: University of Chicago Press.

Callahan, Raymond E. (1975). The American school board, 1789–1960. In *Understanding school boards: Problems and prospects*, edited by P.J. Cistone. Lexington, MA: Lexington Books, pp. 19–46.

Carter, Gene R. and Cunningham, William G. (1997). *The American school superintendent: Leading in an age of pressure*. San Francisco, CA: Jossey-Bass.

Caruso, Nicholas D. (2005). The lone ranger on the board. *School Administrator*, 62, pp. 8–9.
Center for Public Education (2019). *Eight characteristics of effective school boards.* Alexandria, VA: NSBA Publication.
Cistone, Peter J. (ed.) (1975). Understanding school boards: Problems and prospects. Lexington, MA: D.C. Heath & Company, Lexington Books, p. 304.
Creative Effective Lasting (2021). *School board onboarding in 3 simple steps.* Minneapolis, MN: CEL Marketing and PR Design.
D'Angelo, Alexa (2018). *Superintendent changes can impact teachers, students, and community.* Ventura, CA: VC Star (USA Today).
Davidson, Thomas E. (1986). School board/superintendent relations survey. Sponsored by National School Board Association. American Association of School Administrators, and Educational Research Service.
Davis, Jacquelyn (2016). *Improving university superintendent/principal preparation programs: Five themes from the field.* New York, NY: The Wallace Foundation.
Dawson Linda and Quinn, Randy (2000). Clarifying board and superintendent roles. *American Association of School Administrators*, 57, p. 2.
Dawson, Linda and Quinn, Randy (2019). *Good governance is a choice: A way to re-create your board the right way.* Lanham, MD: Rowman & Littlefield Publishers.
Dervarics, Chuck and O'Brien, Eileen (2019). *Characteristics of effective school boards.* Center for Public Education. Alexandria, VA: National Association of School Boards Publication.
Dlott, Stephen. (2007). *Surviving and thriving as a superintendent of schools.* Lanham, MD. Rowman & Littlefield Education.
Dykes, Archie R. (1965). *School board and superintendent: their effective working relationships.* Danville, IL: Interstate Printers & Publishers.
EAB Education Consulting (2022). *Voice of the superintendent survey.* Washington, DC: EAB Education Consulting.
Eadie, Douglas C. (2003). *Eight keys to an extraordinary board-superintendent partnership.* Lanham, MD: Scarecrow Press.
Endie, Douglas C. (2019). *Building a high-impact board-superintendent partnership: 11 critical questions you need to answer.* Lanham, MD: Rowman and Littlefield Publishers.
Ford, Michael and Ihrke, Douglas (2014). *Yes, school board members are often ideological, and that is OK.* Washington, DC: Brooking Institution.
Fry, Betty, Bottoms, Gene, O'Neill, Kathy, and Walker, Susan (2007). *Schools need good leaders now: State progress in creating a learning-centered school leadership system.* Atlanta, GA: Southern Regional England Board.
Fullan, Michael G. and Stiegelbauer, Suzanne (1991). *The new meaning of educational change.* Toronto: Teachers College Press.
Glass, Thomas E. (1992). *The study of the American school superintendency.* Arlington, VA: American Association of School Administrators.
Glass, Thomas E. (2000). *The study of the American school superintendency 2000: A look at the superintendent of education in the new millennium.* Arlington, VA: American Association of School Administrators.

Goodman, Richard H., Fulbright, Luann, and Zimmerman, Willam G. (1997). *Getting there from here. School board-superintendent collaboration: Creating a school governance team capable of raising student achievement.* Arlington, VA: Educational Research Service & New England School Development Council.

Grissolm, Jason A. and Andersen, Stephanie (2012). Why *superintendents turn over. American Educational Research Journal*, 49(6), pp. 1146–1180. https://doi.org/10.3102/0002831212462622

Gross, Neal C. (1958). *Who runs our schools?* New York: John Wiley & Sons, Inc.

Hackett, Julie L. (2015). *Building relationships, yielding results: How superintendents can work with school boards to create productive teams.* Cambridge, MA: Harvard Education Press.

Hanover Research (2014). *Effective board and superintendent collaboration.* Washington, DC: Hanover Research, District Administrative Practices.

Hanover Research (2020). *Effective superintendent & school board collaboration.* https://www.hanoverresearch.com/reports-and-briefs/

Hentges, Joseph T. (1985). *The politics of superintendent-school board linkages: A study of power, participation, and control.* A presentation to the American Association of School Administrators. Dallas, TX, March 9.

Holmqvist, M. and Lantz Ekström, M. (2024). A systematic review of research on educational superintendents. *Cogent Education*, 11(1). https://doi.org/10.1080/2331186X.2024.2307142

Hunter, Richard C. (2012). *School governance.* Thousand Oaks, CA: SAGE Publication.

Johnson, Paul A. (2010). Leading for learning: Leadership practices for effective boards. *ERS Spectrum*, 28(4), pp. 27–42.

Johnson, Susan Moore (1996). *Leading to change: The challenge of the new superintendency.* San Francisco: Jossey-Bass.

Judge, Timothy, Higgins, Chad, and Cable, Daniel (2000). Employment Interview: A review of recent research and recommendations for future research. *Human Resource Management Review*, 10(4), pp. 383–406.

K-12 Insight (2023). *Report: Big-district superintendents serve longer than commonly thought.* https://www.k12insight.com/news/report-superintendent-tenure/

Kerrins, Judith A. and Cushing, Katherine S. (2001). The classic mistakes of new superintendents. *School Administrator*, 158(2), pp. 8–41.

Kowalski, Theodore (2006). *The school superintendent: Theory, practice, and cases.* Thousand Oaks, CA: Sage Publications.

Kowalski, Theodore (2011). *Public relations in schools.* Upper Saddle River, NJ: Prentice Hall.

Kowalski, Theodore J., McCord, Robert S., Petersen, George J., Young, I. Phillip, and Ellerson, Noelle M. (2011). *The American school superintendent: 2010 decennial study.* Lanham, MD: Rowman & Littlefield.

Kravitz, Robert L. (2023). *To what extent does superintendent longevity relate to student performance as measured by graduation rates.* Seton Hall University Dissertations and Theses (ETDs). https://scholarship.shu.edu/dissertations/3111.

Krosel, Amber, Eads, Audrey, Sherman, Cindy, and Gafner, Jocelyne (2023). *15 things you should do before an interview.* Indeed Career Guide. https://www.indeed.com/career-advice

Levine, Arthur (2005). *Educating school leaders.* Washington, DC: The Education Schools Project.

Lieberman, Myron (1977). Where boards control schools, where they do not – and why? *American School Board Journal,* 164(4), 32–33.

Mannes, John (2015). The problem with our school board. *Education Week,* March.

Marshall, Joanne M., and Ulrich, Jesse D. (2022). *How to keep your superintendent: Board factors related to superintendent turnover.* National School Boards Association. http://works.bepress.com/joanne_marshall/44/

Martin-Kniep, Giselle O. (2012). *Neuroscience of engagement and SCARF: Why they matter to schools.* https://lciltd.org/WebsitePublications/Handbook Neuroleadership EngagementArticleGMK.pdf

McAdams, Donald R. (2006). *What school boards can do.* New York: Teachers College Press.

McCurdy, Jack (1992). *Building better board-administrator relations: A critical review evaluation of the significance of local school leadership and the board-superintendent relationship as a driving force behind it.* Arlington, VA: American Association of School Administrators.

McCurdy, Jack (1993). *Building better board-administrator relations.* Alexandria, VA: American Association of School Administrators, January 1.

McDonald, John (2023). *The role of school boards and superintendents in crisis management.* Framingham, MA: Campus Safety, May.

McGonagill, Grady (1987). Board/staff partnership: The key to effectiveness of state and local boards. *Phi Delta Kappan International,* 69(1), September.

Merz, Carol S. (1986). Conflict and frustration for school board members. *Urban Education,* 20, pp. 397–407.

Metzger, Charles (1997). Involuntary turnover of superintendents. *Thrust for Educational Leadership,* 26(4), 20–22.

National Center for Educational Statistics. https://nces.ed.gov/fastfacts/

National Education Association (2018). *NEA's school crisis guide.* Washington, DC: National Education Association.

National Policy Board for Educational Administration (2015). *Professional standards for educational leaders.* Reston, VA: National Policy Board for Educational Administration.

National School Boards Association (2020a). *How structured interviews help school boards make better superintendent selections.* Alexandria, VA: NSBA Publication.

National School Boards Association (2020b). *The key work of school boards.* Alexandria, VA: NSBA Publication.

New York State Education Department (2015). *Performance standards and rating scale.* Albany, NY: NYSDE.

New York State School Boards Association (2023). *Better school boards lead to better student performance.* New York, NY: New York State School Boards Association.

Pang, Alex Soojung-Kim (2018). *Rest: Why you get more done when you work less.* New York, NY: Hatchette Book Group.

Peetz, Caitlynn (2023). *Education Week*, Superintendent evaluations are murky, incomplete, unfocused. Here's why that matters. April 06.

Poston, William K. (1994), *Making governance work: TQE for school boards.* Thousand Oaks, CA: Corwin Press, Inc.

Price, William (2001). Policy governance revisited. *School Administrator*, 58, pp. 46–48.

Quinn, T. and Keith, M. (2011). *Peak performance governance teams: Creating an effective board/superintendent partnership.* Old Mission, MI: CreateSpace Independent Publishing Platform.

Ray, Harold A. (2003). *ISLLC administrator competencies: A comparison of perceptions among superintendents, school board presidents, and principals* (Doctoral dissertation). Dissertation Abstracts International.

Recker, Leslie. (2022). *How school boards choose a superintendent.* San Diego, CA: Ed100 Publishing.

Reeves, Melissa A., Brock, Stephen E., and Cowan, Katherine C. (2008). *Managing school crises: More than just a response.* Washington, DC: Principal Leadership, National Association of Secondary School Principals.

Rouse, Joseph (2024). *The importance of crisis management and emerging preparedness for superintendents.* Public School WORKS Research and Development Team, Cincinnati, OH: WORKS International.

SageIannaconne, Laurence and Lutz, Frank W. (1970). *Politics, power, and policy: The governing of local school districts.* Columbus, OH: Merrill.

Sergiovanni, Thomas J., Kelleher, Paul, McCarthy, Marthy M., and Wirt, Frederick M. (2004). *Educational governance and administration.* Boston, MA: Pearson Education, Inc.

Sharp, William L. and Walter, James K. (2004). *The school superintendent: The profession and the person.* Lanham, MD: Scarecrow Education.

Shelton, Thomas (2015). *Transforming beliefs into action. Board and superintendent teams working together. Improving school board effectiveness: A balanced governance approach*, Cambridge, MA: Harvard Education Press, pp. 33–42.

Smoley, Eugene R. (1999). *Effective school boards: Strategies for improving board performance.* San Francisco, CA: Jossey-Bass Publishers.

Story, Ashley (2023). *Closing the deal and getting real: Superintendent contract negotiations and evaluations.* Columbia, SC: White and Story LLC, Attorneys at Law.

Tallerico, Marilyn (1988). *The dynamics of the superintendent-school board relationship* (A Doctoral Dissertation). Arizona State University.

Thompson, Ray, Templeton, Nathan, and Ballenger, Julia (2013). School board presidents and superintendents' use of transformational leadership to improve student outcomes. *National Forum of Educational Administration and Supervision Journal*, 30(4), p. 1.

Togneri, Wendy and Anderson, Stephen E. (2003). *Beyond islands of excellence: What districts can do to improve instruction and achievement in all schools.* Washington, DC: Learning FIrst Alliance.

Townsend, Rene S., Johnston, Gloria L., Gross, Gwen E., Lynch, Peggy, Garcy, Lorraine M., Roberts, Benita B., and Novotney, Patricia B. (2007). *Effective superintendent-school board practices: strategies for developing and maintaining good relationships with your board.* Thousand Oaks, CA: Corwin Press.

U.S. Department of Education. https:// nces.ed.gov/fastfacts/

U.S.Government Accountability Office (2022). *Annual report.* Washington, DC: U.S.Government Accountability Office.

Van Der Bogert, Rebecca and King, Matthew (1999). *Partner in progress: strengthening the superintendent-board relationship.* San Francisco, CA: Jossey-Bass, Inc. Publishers.

Van Deuren, Amy E., Evert, Thomas F., and Lang, Bette A. (2015). *The board and superintendent handbook: Current issues and resources.* Lanham, MD: Rowman and Littlefield Publishers.

Van Deuren, Amy E., Evert, Thomas F., and Lang, Bette A. (2016). *Working toward success: board and superintendent interactions, relationships, and hiring issues.* Lanham, MD: Rowman and Littlefield Publishers.

Walter, James K. and Carlan, Catherine (1998). *Telltale warning signs of imminent danger for the school superintendent.* Alexandria VA: Board & Administrator, July.

Wirt, Frederick M. and Kirst, Michael W. (1997). *The political dynamics of American education.* Berkeley, CA: McCutchan.

Ziegler, L. Harmon, Jennings, M. Kent, and Peak, G. Wayne (1974). *Governing American schools: Political interactions in local school districts.* North Scituate, MA: Duxbury Press, p. 269.

Index

Note: Please note that the page locators in italics refer to tables.

24/7 information, 62

accountability, 22, 24, 28, 31, 33, 48, 81, 82, 90
accurate information, 35
administrative team/cabinet members: authoritarianism, 87; cabinet's agenda, 85–86; micromanagement, 87; modern superintendency, 85; one-person operation, 85; superintendent roles, 86
advanced degree stipend, 16
advanced placement (AP) classes, 41
ambassadors, 44
American Association of School Administrators, 16
American Civil War, 73
American philosopher, 101
American politician, 5, 51
American taxpayers trust, 48
Anderson, Stephen E., 83
annual salary, 15, 17, 18
annual salary rate, 15
Arkansas, Georgia, Indiana, and North Carolina, 104
athletic events, 69
athletics, 43, 44, 66

attitudes, 10
attorney-at-law, 14
authoritarianism, 87
author's thoughts on the scenarios, 113–22
automobile allowance, 16

beliefs, 10, 44
benefits of job: superintendent's contract, 15; tax-sheltered annuities, 15–16; vacation and sick leave, 15
Blackburn, Barbara R., 62
Blumberg, Arthur, 40
board committees, 37, 66
board meetings, 22, 23, 32, 36–38, 40, 62, 63, 65–67, 82, 86, 97, 117
board-savvy superintendents, 86
bonus, 16
Boston pattern of governance, 1
Bottoms, Gene, 105
Buechler, Carl W., 102
Bureau of Labor Statistics, 81
bus routes, 43
buyout clause, 18–19

cabinet's agenda, 85–86
cafeteria, 43

Carlan, Catherine, 96
Caruso, Nicholas D., 32
Center for Public Education, 23, 24
Center for Public Education's study, 82
Center for Reform of School Systems, 33
Cherokee Nation, Indian Territory, 47
chief financial officer, 29, 52
classic mistakes, 10
coercion, 75
coherent governance, 76–78
collaborative bargaining, 52, 53, 54
collaborative or interest-based bargaining model, 53
colonial period, 1
Colorado, 104
command team, 91
communication: board meetings, 36; elections, 36; frustration and tension, 36–37; lack of, 35; leadership team, 37–38; media, 63–64; needs and expectations, 36; orientation binder, 37; roles of board, 37
communication protocols, 91
community attitude, 52
community relations: communication, staff and community, 43; district's education program, 43; first-hand knowledge, 44; key communicators, 43, 44; misperceptions and rumors, 44; problem-solving, 43, 45; role of superintendent and school board members, 43; social media, 44
community service organizations, 16
community stakeholders, 90–92
compensation, 15
comprehensive interview, 6
confidentiality, 7, 121
conflict/power struggles: contract obligations, 58; differences, individual board members, 58; disagreements, 58; partnership, 57–58; poor leadership, 57; public discussions, 57; recommendations, 58; students' welfare, 57

confusion, 31–33, 39, 45, 82, 114
conservatism, 1
coping, 89
creative compensation ideas, 16–17
crisis management: causes, 89; coping and problem-solving abilities of students, 89; disaster recovery, 90; plan, 90–92; protection, students, teachers and staff, 90; safety and security, schools, 90; school violence, 90; suburban school district, 92
crisis management team, 91
Cushing, Katherine S., 10
cycle of poverty, 102

data-driven decision-making: components, 81; high and lower-performing districts, 82–83; implementation, 81; macro-level visions, 81; measures, 81; newspaper, 83; processes, 81–82; public comment, 83; sharing information, 82
data-driven insights, 82
Davis, Jacquelyn, 105
Dawson, Linda, 32, 43, 76, 77
deliberate rest, 69
Department of Education sites, 104
design firm, 37
disability of superintendent, 18
disaster recovery, 90
dishonor, 10
dismissal, 49
District Accountability Committee (DAC), 66–67
district's communication plan, 37
district's education program, 43
Dlott, Stephen, 52
duties and responsibilities for superintendents, 14–15, 22, 31
dysfunctional leadership: administrators and teachers, 47; decision-making process, 48; effective and ineffective school governance, 48; executive session, 49; knowledge and expertise,

47; mid-1930s, 47; national education reform, 48; "perfect-fit," 47; role of elected board members, 48; school districts, 47; search for superintendent, 47–48; strategies, 48–49

Eadie, Douglas C., 65, 86
ease of understanding, 82
Edison, Thomas, 69
educational reform, 76
education climate, 76; election communication, 36; good governance, 78; influence, 40; media team, 63; methods, 5; politicians, 40; presidency, 51; quiet, 78; reelection, 110; school board, 36, 40, 74; school board members, 85
Ekström, M. Lantz, 81
electrical engineer, 81
employment, 6, 13
employment-interview research, 6
entrepreneur, 61
environment, 9, 22, 25, 28, 29, 49, 51–53, 89, 92, 105, 122
equity, 39, 41
ethical leadership, 28
expense allowance, 17
extracurricular activities, 44
extra personal/vacation days, 17

Facebook, 92
face-to-face interview, 8
father of American literature, 61
father of American psychology, 101
federal governments, 44
Ford, Michael, 39
Ford Motor Company, 61
frustration and tension: board members, 35–36; superintendent's, 35–36
Fry, Betty, 105

gender identity, 40
governance: administrative recommendations, 76–77; coercion, 75; coherent, 76–78; coherent governance model, 77–78; complexity, 76; critics, 74; educational reform, 76; education climate, 76; election, 78; exit interviews, 76; financial and legal issues, 74; functioning without commitment, 74–75; functioning without ground rules, 75; issue's contribution, 75; kid issues, 77; local school district, 73; making policy-level decisions, 77; making political decisions, 74; mistakes, 74–75; neglecting self-improvement, 75; personnel and student discipline, 76; policy, 76; public education, 74; public's interest, 73; purpose and function of board, 77; quality of, 76; responsibility, 73; school board's goal, 73–74; vision, 77
guaranteed annual salary, 17

Hackett, Julie L., 21
Hanover Research, 2
health and life insurance, 16
hiring: decisions, 6; process of, 5; request for proposal, 6–7; strategies, 10–11; superintendent, 5; survey, 7
historical perspective: 1800s school systems, 1; colonial period, 1; conflict, superintendents and boards, 1–2; conservatism, 1; early superintendents, 1; relationships, superintendent-school board, 2; seventeenth century, 1
Holmqvist, M., 81

ideologically driven politics: AP classes, 41; challenges, 39–40; debates, 40; elected school boards, 39; local government, 39; national survey, 39; newspapers, 40; school board elections, 40
Ihrke, Douglas, 39
Illinois, 104

incident command system (ICS), 91
indemnity clause, 17
Internet, 62
interviews: common interview missteps, 8–9; comprehensive, 6; confidentiality, 7; determinations of "fit," 5; elimination and compromise, 7–8; employment, 6; exit, 76; face-to-face, 8; media, 63; process, 5–8; screening, 6; student participation, 7; suggestions, 8; types of questions, 6
Irish, 1

James, William, 101
Jeff, 102
job: determinations of "fit," 5; requirements of, 5
journalism/journalists, 61, 62

K-12 public education, 48
K-12 schools, 90
keeping your bags packed: board problems for the superintendent, 96–97; future of superintendency, 98; "perfect fit" district leader, 98; political base, 95–96; public education, 98; risk for termination, 96; tenure of superintendent, 95, 96; vote to dismiss, 95; warning signs, 96–98
Kennedy, John F., 51
Kerrins, Judith A., 10
key communicators, 43, 44
key people, 62
Kouzes, Jim, 102
Kowalski, Theodore J., 32, 61
Krosel, Amber, 8

lack experience, 32
lack of communication, 35
lack of competence, 2
lack of crisis management training, 89
lack of leadership, 47
lack of stakeholder participation, 64
lack of trust and mutual respect, 21
lack of understanding, 75
language, 14–18
laptop, 16
leadership organizational chart, 37
Leader's Legacy, A, 102
legacy: agenda, 101; challenges, 102; late nineteenth century, 101; long-term, 101, 102; superintendent's role, 101; time to build and leave, 101; vocation of teaching, 101–2; what is your "why?", 102
Levine, Arthur, 105
life insurance supplement, 17
Lincoln, Abraham, 73
listening, 10
local government, 39
local law enforcement, 92
logistics, 91

macro-level visions, 81
marketing, 37
McAdams, Donald R., 33
McCurdy, Jack, 32
McGonagill, Grady, 2
media: 24/7 information, 62; asset or liability, 61; challenges, 61–62; communication, 63–64; coverage, 63; fast-breaking information, 62; information-based society, 61; interview, 63; key points, 62–63; negative news, 61, 62; nerve-wracking pace of decision-making, 61; outlets, 62; public education, 61; social, 44; superintendency, 61; traditional, 63
medical plan premiums, 16
Merz, Carol S., 2
micromanagment, 74, 87
misperceptions, 44
mistakes, 10, 74–5
modern superintendency, 85
The Monk Who Sold His Ferrari, 89
motivations, 31, 32
mutual agreement, 18

National School Boards Association, 5, 22, 36, 81
negative behaviors, 21
negative news, 61, 62
negotiating superintendent contracts: attorney-at-law, 14; board's legal representative, 13; cognizant of the interests, 14; complex nature, 19; description, 13; elements, 14–19; process, 13–14; terms and conditions of employment, 13; time to review, 19; veteran administrator's contract, 19
newspaper, 40, 61, 83
New York State Education Department, 25
non-traditional benefits: automobile allowance, 16; professional membership dues, 16; technological devices, 16
NSBA Key Work of School Boards, 25

Oklahoma, 47
onboarding, 36 38, 49
O'Neill, Kathy, 105

Pang, Alex Soojung-Kim, 69
parents and community members, 39
parking lots, 43
partnership, 57
Peetz, Caitlynn, 24
pension system, 16
perfect fit district leader, 98
personnel and student discipline, 76
philosophy, 85
planning, crisis management: collaboration with community, 91; communication protocols, 91; crisis management team, 91; ICS, 91; procedures, 92; regular training, 91; risk assessment, 90–91
planning team, 91
policies, school board, 37
poor communication, 35
poor leadership, 57
Posner, Barry, 102

preconceptions and biases, 10
print media, 62
professional development, 17
professionalism or integrity, 17, 57
professional membership dues, 16
Professional Standards for School Leaders, 6
public board meetings, 38
public education, 61, 74, 98
Public Records Act, 36
public relations, 31, 37
public's interest, 73
publisher, 61

Quinn, Randy, 32, 43, 76, 77

race, 39–41
radio, 62
Recker, Leslie, 7
reports, journalists', 61
request for proposal (RFP), 6–7
researchers, 31, 32
retirement plan contributions, 16
retirement programs, 16
risk: assessment, 91; biases, errors and personal preferences, 6; continuous improvement, 21; *versus* rewards, 98; termination, 96
Rogers, Will, 47
Rouse, Joseph, 93
rumors, 35, 44, 116

safety and security, schools, 90
salary factors, 15
school board: challenges, 39–40; dysfunction, 48; elections, 40; meetings, 40. *See also* standing committees; structure, 65
school district: community relations, 43, 44; goals, 45
school-improvement initiatives, 64
school management, 31
school safety, 39–40
school violence, 90
screening interview, 6

shared knowledge, 36
sharing information, 82
sick leave, 15
smartphone, 16
Smoley, Eugene R., 74
social media, 44
Socrates, 95
stakeholders, 7, 10, 22, 63, 81, 90, 92, 106
standard performance evaluations, 17
standing committees; DAC participants, 66–67; governance, 65–66; key characteristics, 65; participants' roles, 66; role of superintendent, 66, 67; structure, 65; suggestions, 66
State Association of School Administrators, 16
State Department of Education, 66
state governments, 44
Story, Ashley, 14
stress, 8, 61, 69, 70
student achievement, 43
students' best interests, 36
sub-committee, 63
succeeding, 10, 18
successful superintendents, 98
superintendent: advice, 33; challenges, 39–40; communication. *see* communication; district performance, 33; frustration and tension, 36–37; opinions of, 32; politics, 40; responsibilities, 33; role confusion, 32; school management, 31; survey, 103–6
superintendent contract elements: benefits, 15–16; buyout clause, 18–19; compensation, 15; creative compensation ideas, 16–17; duties and responsibilities, 14–15; indemnification clause, 17; performance evaluation, 17–18; term, 14; termination, 18
supplemental retirement plan, 16

survey, 7
survey data: design, 104; district leaders, 105; "keep your bags packed," 105–6; online, 104; policies, 103; practicing superintendents, 123–26; purpose of, 103; scale, 105; school district's vision and mission, 104; summary table, *126–27*; superintendent preparation programs, 106; superintendent-school board relationships, 104–5; training, 105; valuable recommendations, 105

tablet, 16
tax-sheltered annuities, 15–16
teacher contract negotiations: challenges, 32–33; collaborative bargaining, 53, 54; district's negotiation team, 32; implementation, 31; local contract negotiation, 31; meetings, 31; school districts, 31; sessions, 34; traditional or adversarial bargaining, 31–32; veteran teacher, 34; win-win negotiation, 52
teacher's job, 58
technological devices, 16
television, 62
termination, 14, 18, 96, 97, 108
term of contract, 14
thought-provoking scenarios, 107–11
Togneri, Wendy, 83
torts, 17
town hall meeting, 45
traditional media, 63
traditional model, 39
training, 49
transparency, 24, 28, 36, 37, 82
trends, 16, 22, 82
trust and mutual respect: annual board self-evaluation, 24–25; building effective, 21; communication and community relations, 28–29; effectual governance and school system management, 25; efforts, 21–24; governance team,

24; lack of, 21; negotiation session, 29; NYSED states, 25; performance standards and rating scales, 28; pre-assessment meeting, 28; public education, 24; seasoned veteran, 21; successful boards, 25
trustee role, 32
trustworthy, 11
truth, 43

United States, 1, 5, 39, 51, 61, 73, 101
unused vacation/sick days payment, 16
U.S. Census Bureau, 81
U.S. Government Accountability Office, 90
U.S. history, 1
U.S. territories, 90

vacation leave, 15
value-added perspective, 10
veteran administrator's contract, 19
veteran teacher, 54
vision, 10, 22, *27*, 28, 37, 47, 48, 62, 64, 75, 77, 81, 103, 104, *126*

vocation of teaching, 101–2
voluntary termination, 18
vote to dismiss, 95

Walker, Susan, 105
Walter, James K., 96
warning signs: contract, salary and evaluation, 96; meetings, 97; superintendent/board/community relationships, 96–97; superintendent's final days, 97
welfare, 2, 57
Western philosophy, 95
Williamson, Ronald, 62
win-lose actions, 10
win-lose negotiating environment, 51–52
win-win negotiation, 52
workaholics, 69
work and home life: deliberate rest, 69; job seldom leaves, 70; overwork, 69; spend time with family, 70; stress, 69; workaholics, 69

yes-women and yes-men, 57

About the Author

John Maloy has worked in public education for four decades. He began his career in Indianapolis, Indiana, as a teacher and coach. During his seventeen years in the MSD Pike Township, Maloy served as an assistant principal and principal at the middle school level. In 1994, Maloy opened a new school designed for the twenty-first century, which served as the first year-round middle school in Indiana. The blueprint created for this school, New Augusta Public Academy, included seven pillars: Elective Enrollment, Cross Campus Collaborations, Personalized Education Plans, Continuous Progress, Parent-School Partnerships, Community and Corporate Partnerships, and an Alternative School Calendar.

In 1997, Maloy accepted a district office position in the Michigan City Area Schools in Michigan City, Indiana, as the assistant superintendent for curriculum, instruction, and assessment before becoming the associate superintendent for personnel and labor relations. After completing his doctorate degree in 2002, Maloy was appointed the superintendent of the Monroe County Community School Corporation in Bloomington, Indiana. Four years later, Maloy accepted the role of assistant superintendent for the Aspen School District in Aspen, Colorado. In 2010, Maloy transitioned into the superintendent position before retiring in 2019. Today, he maintains a passion for public education and seeks alternative pathways that will ensure success for students, teachers, and educational leaders.

Maloy was awarded the Olin Davis Award for Exemplary Teaching of Economics from the Indiana Council for Economic Education in 1986. From 2003 to 2006, he received the following accolades from the Chamber of Commerce: Healthy Business Award for Investing in the Health of Employees, Leading Light Award for Community Partners in Reading, and Environmental Award for Contributions to the Health & Safety of the Community.

In 2005, Maloy received the Dean F. Berkeley Emerging Leadership Award from Indiana University, School of Education.

Maloy earned his Ed.D. and Ed.S. from Indiana University Bloomington in Educational Policy & Leadership, his M.S. in Secondary Education from IUPU Indianapolis, and his B.S. in Secondary Education Social Studies from Butler University in Indianapolis.

www.ingramcontent.com/pod-product-compliance
Lightning Source LLC
Chambersburg PA
CBHW021844220426
43663CB00005B/402